THE LOST MEMOIRS OF A CANADIAN SOLDIER
World War 1 Diary Entries and Letters

Written by Len Willans

Letters and diary entries compiled and transcribed by Gail Booth

Edited by Jennifer Lewis Semchuk

Published by Gail Booth, Kim Brix, and Robert Belland.

Copyright 2012 Bobair Media Inc.

www.LenWillans.com

When my grandfather, Len Willans, passed away, I received his desk. It is small—only two and a half feet wide—with a leaf that folds up to cover all the paraphernalia that a desk collects. It sits hidden around the corner in our laundry room, and I love to sit there and work.

In many ways, it reminds me of my grandfather—neat, compact, unassuming, highly practical, comfortable. That was the grandfather I knew. His desk sat down in a converted greenhouse area attached to their house—away from the bustle of the main house, where he could look out at his beloved flower-filled yard.

We lived on a farm, but Grandpa and Grandma lived only three miles away in our little country village. A trip to town was a big deal and almost always involved a visit to their home. Grandma was outgoing and demonstrative; Grandpa was calm and low key.

I remember walking through his flowerbeds while he explained what each plant was and how it grew. My love affair with flowers probably started there. At other times, I would go down to his "office" to visit and just gaze around at all his books and papers. He was always reading and constantly learning—I think he would have been a real fan of the internet and its educational opportunities. Books and writing still give me a sense of well being and contentment.

Almost always, Grandpa would have his pipe. He never really smoked much of it—just puffed a few times, then pulled out the tobacco and replaced it before relighting it. We used to joke that he didn't smoke a pipe, he smoked matches. The pipe was a prop used to point at things, to demonstrate how something moved or to add emphasis to what he was telling us. The smell of a pipe still brings back memories of him.

Grandpa had a great sense of humour, but it was a droll wit. I did not really appreciate this until I was older because often what he said was so subtle that I did not catch on immediately. When I would finally "get" what he said, I would look at him to find his eyes twinkling and his mouth curved up in a reserved kind of grin.

Grandpa was the local Post Master. Sometimes if there were no other customers, he would unlock the swinging door and let us come inside his work area. Using the long-armed stamper, we would be allowed to cancel out the stamps on a few envelopes, and he would then show us which mailing bags they should go in.

For a number of years, he was the Justice of the Peace for our area—a position that probably called on all of his book learning and life experiences.

But no child ever knows the grandparents as young adults. Working on this project has given me an opportunity to get to know Len Willans as a young man. Grandpa's experiences and his way of relating them speak volumes to the kind of man he was. It has only deepened the love and respect I have for one ordinary and yet very extraordinary man.

We owe a huge debt to him and the millions of others who quietly yet consistently go about their lives with honesty, integrity, and love for their fellow man.

For over 35 years, my Grandfather's World War I memoirs lay in a battered tin box at the back of various storage cupboards in my grandparents' and then my parents' homes. When I finally found them, I knew they were too valuable to sit in the dark, unread; I wanted to share my Grandfather's words with everyone. A compilation of his letters and diary entries from 1916-1918 and his written memoirs from the 1970s, the account you are about to read is told in my Grandfather's words, unembellished and resolutely true to the commitment he felt toward his country and his fellow man.

Gail Booth

Table Of Contents

What follows is intended to be a sketchy view of personal experiences in World War One. It may not be interesting to anyone. It is perhaps an appeal to personal vanity that permits me to put the story on record. Forgive the personal pronouns—the I, I, I—they become unavoidable.

I have written a sober narrative, without embellishment, I believe. I am well aware that many thousands went the same road, with variations.

I can only add that the story is as true as memory—a vivid memory at that—and the aid of a very sketchy diary can make it.

ENLISTMENT

Early in 1915, war fever was high and the Empire was in danger. To enlist in the forces was everyman's duty. My own future was modestly assured as a junior bookkeeper in Garland's Wholesale in Ottawa. I didn't hate anyone and had no desire to kill or even fight.

I presented myself at the Ottawa recruiting office early in 1915, at eighteen, the eligible age. Welcomed there, I explained that I could not enlist unless my mother received the separation allowance for she was dependent upon me. My father was alive but an invalid at 78 years of age. The answer was negative—no allowance was paid while both parents were alive.

In May 1916, the newspapers reported that the enlistment act had been changed and such cases as mine would be taken care of. I wrote to Jess and Arthur (my brothers) and my half-brother Edward in Toronto. Replies, at least, were not negative. Art wired me, "Come to Montreal." He had enlisted in the 148th Montreal battalion associated with McGill University where he had been a divinity student.

On May 22, 1916, I took a Saturday afternoon train to Montreal, had a medical, was sworn in by Art's professor, Major Graham, now padre of the regiment, returned to Ottawa on a night train, and, now in the army, gave my employers a week's notice. The boss had two boys in the forces and applauded my action. I was back the following night in Montreal to report. I was 19.

TRAINING

We were three weeks in Montreal, in Peel Street barracks at the foot of Mount Royal. There, I learned the rudiments of my new trade. Life in Peel Street barracks was not all one's fancy paints. Chiefly, I remember having to fold my blankets in a certain way so that the dark stripe would go straight across the pillow. This was awfully important. Dire results would follow any deviation from the norm. The meals were not what I was used to, ample but coarse. I didn't know then that the cook was a graduate in blacksmithing. Eating from a tin plate offended me. There was a war and of course we must be prepared to suffer!

Then, it was Valcartier Camp, 18 miles from Quebec City, really out in the wilderness—one road in and no road out. Our company, the advance party, arrived in the morning. After a parade to count noses to see that nobody had jumped overboard on the trip, we sat around on the grass with thought of breakfast. It would not require a psychologist to explain why most of the sketchy entries in my diary had to do with food. It was soon evident that we could cancel our ideas about breakfast. The cooks were busy struggling with the unaccustomed job of digging holes and suspending kettles over a wood fire that seemed to produce nothing except smoke signals.

It was about noon when the bugler, who was just learning how to bugle and had been waiting all morning to perform, blew "Cookhouse Door." Then the cooks came up with their supreme effort, a slice of bread and 'mess tin" of beans per man. No butter; something had happened to that in transit. No tea; probably not on the diet sheet. But we were hungry and the beans looked good. The beans would have been very

acceptable had not someone sprayed coal oil on the dying fire and incidentally also sprayed the beans. None of the beans were eaten. We were first in camp and there was no recourse.

Later, we were paraded down a strip of grass marked "C" Company. A lorry dumped off tents a few yards apart down the strip. We were divided into groups of eight to a tent and told to remain. Still hungry, sitting on the grass became tiresome. Soon a tent went up, then another. Without orders, the whole row of tents went up in a straggling line. Someone took notice and gave orders at the top of the line. Tents came down and went up again. The line wasn't much better. This kept up until we were called for supper. By then we were all convinced that a military camp was one grand shemozzle. It was the next day that the top brass took notice. The tents came down again, the area was paced, men were assigned to hold tent poles which were waved into line, and the tents went up to stay.

Valcartier Camp, with the Jacques Cartier River on one side and small mountains surrounding the rest was in splendid isolation and, I suppose, an ideal place to control a young and somewhat rebellious army. Military training was serious enough but simple and uncomplicated. There was little occasion for anything else. Life became a round of guard duties, fatigues, rifle and bayonet training, route marches, practice at the rifle range and instructions in bomb throwing and trench mortars. We were well fed. Breakfast was bacon and beans, bread and butter, and tea; stew and potatoes at noon; bread and jam and sometime rice pudding for supper.

The summer passed quickly and it was common talk that we would soon go overseas.

One incident must be recorded before I quit the Canadian

scene. Every man was entitled to an embarkation leave before departing from Canada. He received a free pass to his home and return and was supposed to have 48 hours at home. Some, who did not want the long trip home, took leave to Quebec or Montreal. In September, my brother Art went to Ottawa and returned before my turn came. He said, "Don't go, Len. There's no fun in it." But I wanted to go and besides, I couldn't refuse without a lot of explanation.

Near the end of the month, I was on my way to Ottawa. Because of train times, I had little more than 24 hours at home. I was glad when it was over. My father, in his late seventies, was confined to the house. When I kissed him goodbye, I knew I would not see him again. My mother was 20 years younger than him but was plainly upset. At that time, many Canadians lay under white crosses in Flanders Fields and others had come home with broken bodies. I suppose, to close relatives, being in uniform seemed like a death sentence. I told myself that I had a priestly father and a saintly mother. That was a quotation I had picked up somewhere but was nevertheless true.

Then there was a girl. Ollie was 16. I was 19. It was no youthful engagement. She was number one girl. I guess I was number one, also. Every lad in uniform was a hero! When I got to other lands, I was thankful that I had that attachment. At least I was faithful to her image.

Embarkation again was the army in action and it seemed as if nobody knew what would happen next. After a long, slow journey on the North Shore Line, time after time we stood on a siding awaiting another train. Once we spent a whole day on a siding somewhere near Bathurst in Nova Scotia. There, we had a route march to counteract ennui. We marched through country lanes where ripe apples overhung the road. When we stopped for the usual five-minute rest, some of the boys started jumping for apples. A house-holder appeared with a bag of ripe apples. He little knew what his kindness would do. Ever since that incident, I have cherished a warm glow for Nova Scotia. That and the returning greeting at Halifax and Truro have remained a fond memory.

We remained for a day in the rail yards at Halifax. I was surprised at the number of Negro families along the water front. Later, I could visualize the devastation caused by the Halifax explosion. We embarked on the Franconia which was some time later torpedoed in the Mediterranean and years later replaced by another vessel of the same name. I was a poor sailor but had plenty of company. Britain owned the seas at that time and we landed in about ten days at Liverpool on October 9, 1916. The visit to England was brief but I did get around.

ENGLAND

I remember being land-sick when we marched along the docks at Liverpool. The first impressions of England, common to most Canadians who were there for the first time, were the funny little trains. Just like the ones in picture books when we were kids, but which we never believed existed except in fairy tales. One of those picture book trains, however, conveyed us to our destination at remarkable speed.

Late in the afternoon, we left the train and marched to Witley Camp. It was dark and raining a little and we stood on a roadside literally for hours until someone found billets for us. If we thought at all, it was about when supper would be ready. When we left the ship, each man was handed one large bun for rations. When we finally got into a hut, we were told to parade for tea. And tea it was. Nothing else. It was then that we realized we had come to a country where food was not plentiful and from then on, how to get enough to eat grew in importance.

Next morning breakfast was on time but in place of the usual beans and bacon each man received a kipper, a slice of bread, and tea. At noon there was stew, usually bully beef, and for supper, bread and watered-down jam and tea. Once in a while, there were extras and some variation but not much of either. Even if one had money, which was also in short supply, there was little in the way of food that could be bought.

The first letters I received in England told of my father's death.

One Sunday afternoon, my brother, Art, and I visited the Witley Parish Church. It was a very old building and has often been mentioned by others. The number of graves in the floor and walls was of peculiar interest. One in particular we thought quaint. Following the name and date in 1641, the squire's third wife slept behind a metal plate in the wall bearing the following verse:

A better woman that here sleeps there's none,

Sara, Rebecca, Rachel, three in one

Religious, pious, thrifty wife, fayre and chaste,

So many goods in one, who finds in haste?

After two weeks at Witley, we packed up and had a route march to Bramshott Camp. That must have been the first time we marched around the Devil's Punchbowl. The march was described as an eight-mile hill. At Bramshott, each man received a shore leave of six days. Art and I decided to use it by visiting Leeds and West Hartlepool. Leeds was our parents' previous home and my father's birthplace, but we had no relatives there. West Hartlepool was the home of my Aunt Annie and two cousins, Fanny and Polly.

October 25, 1916

We arrived in west Hartlepool. We liked our English cousins of West Hartlepool so well that we postponed the Leeds visit and enjoyed a week of bliss with those of like minds and manners—our kith and kin, those who spoke our language and whom we learned to love.

I feel proud of the Hartlepool Willans and I am impressed with the likeness of our mentality. We seemed to understand each other so. We had a delightful time meeting many of our

*cousins and friends; every evening was a "social evening."
We were so busy meeting people that we did not see all the
city but it was a most interesting visit.*

*We visited the aerodrome at Seaton and saw several
"planes" in flight and on the ground. Almost every day a
few "planes" were
over Hartlepool.*

———

On our way back to camp, we spent an afternoon in London.
We visited St. Paul's Cathedral and Westminster Abbey and
saw the Houses of Parliament. But darkness comes early at
that time of year and street lights were dimmed so we were
glad to return to the hostel where we spent the night. In these
first London wanderings, we made acquaintance with the
famed London "Bobby." While we did appreciate the efforts
of the policeman on the beat to help visiting Canadians, much
of the directions we received were wasted. We simply failed
to communicate. Directions like these, "Go right 'head, bear
to the right till you reach King's Way. Cawn't miss it—only
three minutes walk," left us still guessing. In the fading light,
it took somewhat more than three minutes to find our hostel.

Now we were back to camp and work.

I found I had about 20 correspondents and they kept
increasing in numbers. I was busy writing in all my spare
time.

———

October 31, 1916

*Last Sunday night I got lost while out near camp. I
started out at 6 pm to meet Art at the Methodist Church in*

Liphook. He had told me to take the first turn to the right on the Portsmouth Road. I took the turning and after a while reached the Anglican Church. I had only 10 minutes until church time and tried to rectify my mistake by taking a short-cut across country to where I thought the church ought to be.

I followed a path that wound amongst the tombstones through the churchyard and came out into a narrow lane at the other side of the church property. I followed the lane— the night was dark—for a couple of hundred yards where it came to dead end. After hunting about, I found a gate that led me into a wood. Once through the gate, I could see nothing. I was following a path with bushes and trees on either side and had to hold my arms in front of me to shield my face. I travelled that way for over 20 minutes, not knowing where I was or where I was going; for all I knew, I might be going around in a circle. Finally, I landed on a road that took me to Liphook. I am tired of getting lost in that dark, Godforsaken region!

———

Back at Bramshott, there were parades on the common, rifle drill, and a course in trench digging somewhere east of Shottermill village.

———

November 2, 1916

My friend, Gus, and I spent today mending a decayed fire step in one of the bays and when we finished, it was worse than when we started. That is usually the way in the army.

———

But this didn't last.

On November 4, we were again in Witley Camp after marching the eight-mile hill in reverse. I was surely "seeing England" with a pack on my back. We got another look at that freak of nature, the Devil's Punchbowl and had time to study the rough monument erected in memory of the sailor "fowly murdered by highwaymen."

November 14, 1916

The philosophy of the army is that a soldier never works except when he has to and then he does as little as possible. All day yesterday, we worked in the pouring rain, doing a brigade fatigue at the Canadian Ordinance Corps near Liphook. Gus and I were given the job of carting some wood blocks from one place to another. We had no intention of straining ourselves. There was no wheelbarrow, so I invented a hand barrow out of a few slats, and we piled the blocks on it and got to work. There were two corporals to see that we kept at work but I fooled both of them. Gus and I piled the blocks in a square, leaving the center hollow and covering the top with two or three blocks. We managed to make the pile to look pretty big without putting much weight on the barrow. All morning, we kept that up without arousing suspicion.

In the pm, I was sent into a tent to load a truck with tins. After I had finished, I sat down and stayed there until it was time to go home.

At Witley, there were the inevitable days of fatigue duties, night route marches in snow and rain, and other attempts at soldiering. There were field maneuvers on Witley Common, one of them lasting all night, with the usual fish for breakfast—this time, in the form of fish balls, wherein the cook excelled himself, turning out golf balls requiring harsh treatment before eating.

On short notice, most of our company was ordered out in full kit and marched some 14 miles to Mychett Camp for a two-week musketry course. Some of the 107th Battalion went with us. That was November 18th.

November 18, 1916

Again, I am a miserable victim of circumstances, dumped off at this dreary, bleak, Godforsaken hole. I came yesterday, hung up my things, and am quite at home. A number of our boys—a whole hut—about 35 lads—are quarantined with spinal meningitis—the boys don't know that; officially it is called measles. Art and I have been together more or less since I enlisted, until now. But he is on the sick list. I am now away from danger but I have left Art there, and he is ill; I hope he doesn't catch anything.

Gus is in the Bramshott Hospital with a broken ankle bone. He tripped over a pile of stones while answering a false alarm fire call one night.

That march of yesterday was an awful strain especially after the route march of the night before. It was 14 long miles with full pack. The 107th Battalion was with us and they were dropping off like flies. There are a whole bunch of them on the road between Witley and Mychett. No one but

*a strong healthy man can stand such a walk. I only suffered
from my feet and that was because of bad boots but I got new
ones soon.*

I rather liked these route marches. They were a sort of
endurance test. Full kit meant carrying everything the army
issued to you, from rifle and bayonet, entrenching tool, water
bottle, greatcoat, and rubber sheet down to the required
number of hair, boot, and button brushes. Sometimes a
blanket was added. Even without any kit, the march could
sometimes be tough enough. The distance marched, I don't
know. I merely record what we were told at the time. I
certainly never did excel in anything, but for one weighing
125 pounds in my birthday suit, I did prove durable. I didn't
drink or smoke in those days—perhaps that was the answer.

November 18, 1916

*On Friday night, we had a route march with night
operations. We went over to the far side of Thursley
Common and took up a position facing the river Wey.
Captain Scott gave me charge of a sentry group—two men
and myself—and we carried out our part successfully but did
not see the enemy—a band of scouts about 30 in number.*

*Yesterday, for the first time, we had a snow storm. All night,
it rained and now the air is cold, the ground covered with
slush and the whole aspect miserable.*

Mychett Camp was a rifle range with a few huts on a piece of sandy Common Land. Nothing else. We did some shooting and got instructions in rifle care and gas protection but it was hardly serious training. The meals were rough and sketchy. It was just a step closer to the trenches. It was common knowledge that our unit would be broken up to reinforce battalions in France. There had been a payday before leaving Witley and some of the boys found pubs nearby. We had a couple of noisy nights and then all was peace—money all gone. One fellow—Woods—a silly kid, came round with a search light to see if they needed a shave. He stroked their chins and gave a verdict. He told me that he was a barber. I said, "Go, and cut your own hair!"

Sunday was a free day and I spent my time wandering about. I visited Frimley Green and came across the grave of Bret Hart, the poet, in the churchyard of the Frimley Parish Church.

———

November 19, 1916

...From there I continued my walk in a westerly direction, intending to return to Mychett by the first cross-road I came to. But I never came to a cross-road. I walked and walked until I lost myself entirely. I could have found my way back by the way I had come but it would have taken me all evening. I had just started to beg my way back when a taxicab passed me and stopped and one of the two ladies asked me where Mychett was. I told them that that was just what I wanted to know. They told me that they were Mrs. Captain Ogilvie and Mrs. Captain Sewart and seeing that my badge was 148, they invited me into the taxi and I helped the driver find his way to the camp.

At Trimley Church, I got into a conversation with an old man who had been gravedigger for the church for 23 years. He pointed out, with professional pride, all the graves he had dug. He was very interesting. He told me how once he was almost buried alive in a grave he had dug; how once he had buried two people in one grave without anyone knowing it; how, one time, he kept a whole funeral waiting while he dug a grave for the burying.

I saw a number of sod walls that had been laid for a long time; they looked almost like stone, moss covered and damp. I saw a number of big fir trees that had been cut into logs and by "pumping" my friend the gravedigger, I found that they belonged to the local squire and were cut for the government.

———

November 26, 1916

Today, Gibson and I visited Farnborough Abbey. As we came to the Abbey, we stopped at the lodge gates and were directed to a building near the top of the hill. When we got there, a friar came to the door and replied to us in French; then, pointing up the hill, he shut the door. As we went up the hill, the bell was rung to announce our arrival and as we entered the abbey door, we were met by a guide who showed us around. It didn't cost anything to get in; our khaki was a passport but we had to pay to get out. I had to give the guide a shilling and Gibson got stuck for some postcards. In the crypt, we saw the sarcophagus of Napoleon III and the empty one awaiting the Empress Eugenie. The huge stone boxes were said to be of Aberdeen granite and had been presented by Queen Victoria.

On the way back, near a primitive Methodist chapel, printed on a stone in the front of a row of houses were the words, "Read John 3:16." At first, I thought it meant John Read and the number of his house but I have since found out it means, the Gospel of John, chapter 3, verse 16.

At the parish church at Seaton Carew, I saw a little sign tacked up to the effect "Whoever enters here, please give a prayer for the church and its people."

At Mr. Squire's Church, the steward came around with a little plush bag for the offering. I put in all I had—a penny— and it made as much noise as a half a crown.

———

These may sound like simple pleasures but when you draw five shillings a week, your fun is not likely to be riotous.

WAITING TO GO OVERSEAS

December 2, 1916

I was rushed back to Witley on November 29th because another draft was being sent from our battalion. Thirty-five men from each company left December 3 but I am left behind. Art has gone to somewhere in the Midlands to an officer school and will probably get a commission. I feel rather downhearted about Art's going and my being left behind. I hope I will go with the next draft.

I wish I had more money to buy Christmas presents with. I get an average of five shillings a week and it doesn't pay my expenses. I think I will try to get some cards tomorrow to send to West Hartlepool and Canada.

December 3, 1916

I am in number one Y.M.C.A. hut and a service is in progress at the other end of the hut. The boys are singing, "Nearer My God to Thee." I wonder how much nearer I shall be a month from now? I hope I am sent with number 10 Platoon bunch in the next draft. I should like to be with Conlin, Cooke, Hampton, and even Burke.

December 9, 1916

The third draft with number 10 Platoon leaves for France early this week but I am left out again. I am left in C. Coy with Big Tiny, Little Hodges, Cromb, Cheeper, and other misfits.

For five days last week, I had a steady job at trench digging. Every morning, I marched a couple of miles armed with pick and shovel and looked wise until it was time to go home. I learned how to do sod work, construct hurdles of brush, revet caved-in trenches, and handle a lot of little tricks with spade and pick.

Now I have a new job and I have it for a whole week. I am in the brigade post-office as telegraph messenger! After all my training, I have come to this!!! I have to work from 8 am to 8 pm for every day this week but it doesn't look as if I should have much to do.

I have heard from Art a couple of times. He says, "It's left, right, left, right, bloody well left, right all the time." He is evidently as lonely as I am. He says, "Say, sonny. I miss you a great deal, especially in the evening when I do not feel like settling down to work or write letters. We must arrange to meet in London some weekend period." He says all stripes and decoration are removed and a white band is worn around the cap and MPs address him as "Sir." He is treated as an officer but his title is "Cadet."

December 11, 1916

I have found Harry. On Saturday, I found out from a fellow in number four Y.M.C.A. hut that the 51st Battalion was in Whitley but I could not find them. On Sunday, I was sent to the 58th with a telegram; while there, I found out where Harry hung out, but he was not at home. I went with another telegram for Peck of the 51st and while there, I dropped into Harry's hut and called him out. Gee! He was surprised. He looked well and seemed as if the army agrees with him. If I am not on duty, I shall spend Sunday pm with him.

December 12, 1916

At Witley, the 148th had added to some of the 117th Battalion. Recently, part of the 201st Battalion was sent to us but they were taken away again. Yesterday, part of the 171st Battalion was drafted into the 148th. Very few of the original were left.

Our hut is almost deserted. I am left behind with Little Jimmy Hodges, Big Tiny Cunningham, and other misfits.

I have had no pay since I was at Mychett and then only ten shillings. I spent my last shilling on some stuff for my throat which has been "sore" for a couple of weeks. I have exactly 1 penny which is being held for emergency. My pride won't let me borrow, even to post a letter.

December 13, 1916

Draft number three left for France today. A lot of my friends, Chandler, Cooke, Conlin, Evans, have gone with this bunch—all the Lachute and Brownburg boys.

There is a special providence that looks after fools, drunken men and thriftless persons. I was broke the other day and hadn't the money to post a letter and was too proud to borrow. But I found a thripenny bit and a Canadian nickel so now I am on easy street.

December 16, 1916

A fourth draft leaves for France soon but no list is out yet.

Hosky got a card from a friend who is in at Bramshott hospital. He said, "There came pretty near being no more Tobin." He has had pneumonia, I think, or may have been "Spinal McGuinnis."

We had fish balls for breakfast and I think they must have made them out of a piece of shark. The boys called them number 9 pills.

———

Other drafts were being made up. Some of the 117th, 202nd, and 171st battalions were transferred to the 148th. About the middle of December, I was placed on draft for France. I received new webb equipment and from then on, most of our parades were to see that we were all there and ready to go.

I met a chum from Westboro, west of Ottawa. He was with the 51st Battery Light Field Artillery. I spent my last Sunday in England with him and we had our picture taken together. I still have the picture, but the friend, who was later wounded, died some years ago.

While in England, Art, now a corporal, was recommended for a commission in the Flying Corps. In World War One, only commission officers might fly the glorified kites of that time. Shortly after Art left, I got a message from a runner, inviting me to have tea with Major Graham. I shined my buttons and shoes and went. After some questions about myself and family, the Major came to the point. He said he was prepared to recommend me for a commission in the Flying Corps. I was shocked. I knew that officers were drawn from the elite—

mainly college graduates. I protested that apart from my ability to do arithmetic, I had no education.

He then suggested that I take an N.C.O.'s course. Faced with this, I found I didn't want to get off the draft. The Major was insistent, but while I thanked him for his intentions, I elected to go with my comrades. It was common knowledge that we were soon leaving for France; in fact, my name was on the next draft. I was packed up ready to go any day and that is what I had enlisted for. I declined his well-meant offers with appreciation. He asked me to think it over and he seemed rather hurt. He probably decided that I wasn't so bright after all. Oddly enough, I did end up in the Flying Corps.

———

December 20, 1916

These are the days of indecision. Last Friday—five days ago—I was ordered to go on a draft overseas. I have received my Webb equipment, packed my stuff, put my house in order: and now I am not sure that the draft will go at all! Captain Graham is using all his influence to keep me off the draft. He wants me to be an N.C.O., and even if the draft goes, I may not go. It depends on Captain Scott.

I wired Art that I was to be going and he replied, "Get off, if possible. Graham will help you." I had written him explaining that I wrote to Fanny that I was going, also Mother and Olive – and now I am not sure if I'm to go or not.

The doubtfulness of the business has got on my nerves. I cannot help worrying about what acquaintances will think of me for not writing and for making incorrect statements to my family.

If I don't hear anything further, I'll write to Mother, Olive,
Art, and Fanny to the effect that I am not leaving at present.

Finally, on December 22 at 5:15 am, I left Witley Camp to Milford, to Southampton, to Havre, for the Base. We spent all day in Southampton doing fatigues. We helped load some mail in one boat but mutinied because we had to work in a dirty, dusty hold and we got away with it.

I enlisted May 22, 1916, arrived at Liverpool October 9, arrived in France December 23, 1916, and went into the front line trenches mid-January, 1917. Those dates are inserted to show the period of training before an infantryman was considered ready to fight for his country. Eight months from the office desk to the front line.

My saga really begins in France. The eight months of preparation was a routine matter of common interest. Although I started to tell of what happened to one individual Canadian in Flanders, I felt that I must relate how he got there.

Early on the morning of December 22nd, 1916, we left Witley, entrained at Milford to Southhampton and arrived at Le Havre on December 23rd.

On December 23, 1916, we left Southhampton at 6:00 p.m. on a side-wheeler and arrived at Le Havre during the night. I think most of us were sea-sick. The crossing was rough and the zig-zag course of the little ship, to avoid subs, didn't help. I got no relief until the terrible motion ceased; then I went to sleep. We were roused before dawn. Twenty of us remained to clean ship. The rest marched off. It was still rough, even in the harbor. The tub rolled badly and as we were about to bid it goodbye, the gangway slipped off the dock, was splintered, and fell into the harbor. We had a couple of hours' wait until a small vessel came alongside. It was tricky getting aboard in full kit, the waves were high, and our old tub was a side-wheeler. We finished by climbing a rope ladder to the quay; then we marched through Havre.

The little town left two impressions as we marched through: two butcher shops, one for mutton and beef and one for horse meat. We marched through the town and then got on a streetcar which took us within a mile of the Canadian Base.

This was a training area where we stayed for a month.

We were on a plateau above Le Havre, France, which was said to house some 14,000 troops. There were a few square miles of tents and at this time of year, it was mud—mud everywhere.

December 24, 1916

This is the worst mud-hole in Europe. We have only been there 24 hours and we are plastered from head to foot with soft, gluey, mud.

Immediately upon arriving, we had a rapid medical examination; then we received a rifle, bayonet, sling, gas-helmet, and rifle cover.

We slept ten men to a bell tent, wood floors coated generously with mud. Clothes were muddy, and so were the blankets. We didn't undress; even the boots, when removed, were double their weight with mud. A gas respirator was added to our equipment. Reveille was at 4:30 a.m., parade at seven.

The training was not new—bayonet-fighting, bomb throwing, and physical jerks by some bored instructors who had seen active service. Rations were pretty slim and we lived in the mud for it rained most of the time.

I did take a Sunday afternoon pass to visit Le Havre but didn't stay long. I walked down the one main street, all hill—Rue de Gallion. One side of the street was a row of brick houses, all brothels, licensed and inspected by the French government. It was a lasting impression which coloured my opinion of France for a long time

I remember thinking, Christmas tomorrow! I spent my birthday in one country and now Christmas in another.

December 28, 1916

I didn't have a very merry Christmas: it was rather a miserable Christmas.

What a Christmas! Raining lightly, parade at seven. Then a route march, a few miles up paved road and back again. The rest of the day was free. We spent the time crowded in the tent, rain and mud outside, mud and rain inside. The tent was a sieve.

December 28, 1916

One must have good teeth to live here. Every day we go up on the mountain to train, and at noon, we have dry rations issued. One day we got tea—weak and weedy—cheese, a tin of jam amongst six—and dog biscuits. Those biscuits are some dope—hard as leather, and brittle as glass—but – "they are good food for soldiers." When we get to the front, we will line dug-outs with them, for they will surely be bomb-proof. At present, we are considering the desirability of paving our street with them.

Of course we sleep in tents and lovely it is! There are wooden floors in our tents but it is a cold proposition to sleep on those floors in winter. In the morning, when we roll out at 4:30, the inside of the tent is coated with frost and our top blankets are wet with frost. We have our own rifles and gas-helmets. We use our rifles for foot warmers—rather frozen warmers.

Carry on!

December 29, 1916

At present, as I have mentioned, I am at the Canadian Base near Havre but there is some talk of us moving to Boulogne or somewhere else near there. If we do, I shall see some more of France. Of course, I might go up the line the next week, probably to the Somme District.

There is a Hun detention camp here but I think it is only a temporary one. I overheard a chat with Fritz the other day.

A Cockney was passing and called out, "Hello, Fritz, you are headed to prison camp. The Hun was quite ready to talk in broken English. He informed us that, "The war is fineeeshed."

December 30, 1916

This morning, we went through "gas." Just before the ordeal, the mouth-piece of my helmet fell out. I got it fixed up again but not very securely for when I went through the gas-room I got a mouthful of the stuff but I grasped the space around my mouth and hurried through.

December 31, 1916

Instead of going to church parade as I had hoped, I spent the morning carrying buckets of mud off the mess room street. 'Tis an awful war!

This is the last of a year, six months of which I have lived in khaki—not the happiest part of my life but certainly the most varied.

I never loved the army. I have hated it and all it meant since the first day I slept in the barracks yet I had no misgivings as to the future. I enlisted because I believed it the right thing to do—and I am more certain now that I was right.

We are fighting a people who have committed a great wrong and we have to win. The British slogan in victory or adversity is "just carry on." I do not fear death; yet I am young and want to live; but I am willing to give all I have—my life— that wrong may be rectified; that is because of my hope in a life to come.

I have been practicing Christian Socialism since we came to France and found it works. If ever I come out this war alive, I shall have an irrefutable argument to back up Christianity.

We, the British, are in every way superior to our enemies. In men, we have a great advantage—more men and better trained men. In that of second importance—artillery—we lead by a huge majority both in guns and ammunition. Even in such things as bombs, gas, and liquid fire, we have got the upper hand.

It is my firm conviction that if the war does not end by next June, it will be won on the West Front.

The Canadian Base I cannot begin to describe. It is part of five miles of camps. It is not very large—only holds about 14,000 Canucks. The long line of camps is situated in a valley well protected from aerial raids, high above the sea, awfully muddy; the training camps are upon a hill on one side of the valley. All troops are under canvas; we have a wooden floor in our tent, but the tent leaks like a sieve. There is not a level spot in camp; all is mud and hill and then more mud.

Tomorrow is the New Year. I shall be glad when another new year comes. I have a new diary which I shall start to use on the morrow.

January 3, 1916

On the last day we were up on the hill, we had a competition in Physical Training between Imperial troops and Canadian troops. In a relay race between 20 Canadians and the same number of Imperials, we beat the Imperials by a man and a half. In an obstacle race between about a thousand of each, we beat the Imperials by a large majority. They were good sports; whenever we won, they cheered us in a hearty British way. It was evident the Canadians sent now are of an average better than the present English Tommies.

For five days a week, our routine started with parade at seven, "Up the Hill," a short route march to the training area.

This kept up until January 18. Then we were held in readiness to go up the line. The only release was a weekly evening pass to visit Le Havre, where estaminets and brothels were ready to welcome the troops. On the night of January 11, we had a Zepp raid alarm which failed to materialize. Lights were out all night. I was on an armed detail which found nothing to do and so did nothing.

Now I was on a draft to go "up the line." On January 20, we left camp for Le Havre at 5:45 p.m. then left Le Havre at 12:30 a.m. on January 21, packed in small box cars bearing the soon-to-be familiar legend "Hommes 40-Cheveaux 8." I haven't forgotten, "Horses 8, Men 40." There wasn't room to lie down except with your head on one man's chest and your legs across another. After parts of two days, stopping and starting, we got out near Neuville St. Vaast, a shell-shocked town with a church steeple that looked ready to fall any time and marched to Hermanville.

I was now one of a party of 19, reinforcements to the 60th Battalion. We slept in a loft over some bakery ovens. It was warm, but the arched brick floor was something to which the human frame could not conform. There were about 40 lads in the loft, practically all strangers. I didn't know anyone. We all wanted to lie down, something we hadn't been able to manage in the box car. They were good lads, all in the same boat. We solved the situation by piling our kit on the humps and lying in the hollows, each man half on the next.

We did get out for the "ovens" briefly and found evidently the only civilian there, an old French woman living in a cellar under a shattered house and conducting, of all things, a canteen! A comrade and I pooled our resources and bought what we thought was a can of ham. Deceived by the flickering candle, it opened up to be a can of string beans! We ate them anyway—anything to get away from bully and hardtack.

Several parcels of Christmas mail caught up with me that night. They were intended for Art and I, but I was headed for the front line next day. To burden myself needlessly was asking for trouble and would probably decrease my chance of survival. I opened all parcels, packed what goodies I could in pack and haversack and gave the rest away to all comers with a free hand. Candy, cake, and cigarettes found ready recipients.

Next evening, the roll was called, and a number of groups formed. We marched at dark to the trenches. After a half mile overland, we dropped into a trench. I followed the leader but couldn't see the bottom of the trench and put my hand out on white "stone" to break my fall. The "stone" came loose in my hand. It was a human skull, evidently put there as a guide. I shoved it back in place and said, "Stay there, old man." Some fool things you don't forget.

On January 24, we went through a gas room to test our respirators, then had a rest until evening and lined up at dusk to go into the trenches. It was a black winter's night. We marched past the Mont St . Eloi Church and then in single file followed a guide overland for a mile or so before seeking the security of a trench. It was cold, a couple of inches of snow on the ground, but a clear night. The enemy's brilliant parachute flares lighted the sky ahead. The occasional gun fired, a shell burst somewhere in front, and the chatter of machine guns broke the silence once in a while.

Our party split up, some to one platoon, some to another. I found myself in number nine platoon of "C" Company. I was escorted to a front line dugout and handed over to a corporal. He sent me down the dugout to rest "until your relief calls you." I was to be gas-guard at the dugout entrance, three hours on and three off. Three or four men were asleep on the hard-pounded floor. A stub of candle showed me the way. I couldn't sleep and dearly wanted to ask questions, but nobody was interested. The candle burned out, and I lay in the dark wondering "What next?" Scared? No, just curious. I was almost asleep when someone clambered down the stairs and struck a match. It was my mate, Tom, on the job. He had red hair and a trace of Scottish accent.

He followed me up the stairs and passed on his instructions, then left me and said to wake him up in three hours. I had to challenge any movement– (the password was "Quebec") and warn those below of any gas or other happenings. The three hours on and three off I found hard to take. At first I couldn't sleep and then slept like one drugged. The night passed quietly enough, with once in a while a bomb or trench mortar to the right or left and the whistle of a few bullets overhead. At dawn, the platoon officer came by. He answered my challenge with, "So you're the new man?" At dawn, an officer and sergeant came with the rum ration. He unslung a rum jar but I refused. "Oh, you'll soon take it," he said. I had never tasted rum. By the second day, I refused nothing that was offered. Rum was only served on the front line. As they left, a fatigue party came with rations, one-quarter of a two-pound loaf for the day, one rasher of bacon, and a mess tin of tea.

He told me that we were on a bit of a salient and that a converted naval gun could enfilade our trench. "If he starts throwing them over, better stand inside the doorway. Lad was killed here yesterday on this job," pointing to a part of the parados blown away. The others came up from the dugout for their rum. I was somewhat nonchalant about the lad killed there yesterday. I told myself that lightening never strikes in the same place twice. I hadn't lived long enough to know what a lie that is.

By noon, the job became routine. It was "a quiet day on the Western Front."

It was well on in the afternoon when I heard the gun. As I was not alert to all sounds, I heard the distant "pop" followed by the whine of an approaching shell which became a freight-train roar as it went overhead. It burst perhaps half a mile away. So, this was the naval gun I had heard about? I was still considering the incident when I heard the gun again. This time, the shell seemed to come streaming right at me. I saw a geyser of frozen mud erupt about a hundred yards away. "Guess I'd better step inside."

Normally one would back into the small square hole of the dugout entrance and proceed crab-wise down the steps. I probably intended to reach the second step where at least my head would be under cover and clumsily tried to step down face forward encumbered with a bayoneted rifle. The rifle proved awkward and slowed my movements. There was an earthquake behind me. That was one shell I never heard. It landed just over the back of the trench, and I found myself on the floor of the dugout with a couple of fellows helping me up and asking if I was hurt. I insisted that I wasn't hurt although I was probably bruised all over. I had fallen only a dozen steps and was still clutching my rifle. My whole body reacted like a plate of jelly but I crawled up the stairs immediately for my pride was hurt. I spent the next couple of hours dodging in and out of the doorway and developed a healthy regard for high explosive shells. I was learning fast!

I had discovered by now that I was in the 60th Battalion. Nobody had even heard of the 148th! Between then and the Battle of Vimy Ridge, there were many trips in the line. We made six-day trips, front line, then support line—200 yards back—then reserve line, half a mile back. We were below and facing the ridge, where the enemy occupying the height, could look right into our trenches. Not a happy position to be in.

January 29, a Monday, I was asleep on the dugout floor

when something happened. The Huns had been sending over a few trench mortars, run jars (mostly shrapnel) and minnies, big babies with a lively wallop. Minnies—the Hun name was Minnenwerfer (mine thrower). The repeated thumps overhead had just made me wake up when a minnie landed on our dugout and caved in the stairway. The blast had put out the candle and filled the place with choking white smoke. It appeared at first that we were completely buried but as the smoke cleared, a ray of light could be seen up the stairway. We were alive. The corporal produced a shovel. Gasping for breath, we took turns at scraping away dirt, stones, and pieces of plank.

We had worked feverishly for the rest of the dugout might collapse at any time. Soon we had a narrow tunnel to the open air. It was the corporal's job to get us out safely. The serenade of hate above continued. The instructions were, "one at a time. Turn right and run to the first C.T. Go to the Platoon headquarters dugout up the C.T." All got away safely. That night we were relieved by the 52nd Battalion.

My second trip was in support line. There, we spent the days hunched in crude shelters and our nights on working parties. This latter was usually digging out some trench blown in the night before. Our work was interrupted by occasional "whiz-bangs." This was a light shell filled with steel marbles—nasty little things that seemed to travel faster than the speed of sound.

We spent February 1st and 2nd building a trench parapet near the front line. We drew some machine gun fire and spent more time tumbling into the trench than we did working. The day was usually quiet, for planes were up with anti-aircraft guns active and the occasional "dogfight" up above.

One of these working parties was at The Tunnel. The Tunnel was something! The tunnelers had constructed this underground passage from back in the reserve area to within a short distance of the front line, equipped with a light railway, which later brought up rations and ammunition and took back the wounded. They slowed operations when they discovered that the enemy was making a similar tunnel almost directly opposite. In April, when the Battle of Vimy was at its height, they worked through to the enemy tunnel and had an underground road through to the enemy's road before the ridge was taken!

Working at the tunnel wasn't fun. We would crawl down the entrance, carry up a bag of chipped limestone and take it some distance to unload, so as not to mark the entrance with white stones. We would "freeze" when an enemy flare went up, for movement would draw fire, and flop when the odd burst of machine gun fire came our way. It was hard work, and scary too, all night.

Then it was back in the front line, still Neuville St. Vaast front but a different sector. When on a machine gun post, it was three on, three off. Three men would take turns standing on the fire-step, watching. We were warned to "freeze" when the Huns sent up a flare. "He can't see you unless you move." I froze and got a good view of No Man's Land.

It was the same day and night, except that we used a simple periscope in daylight, two bits of mirror about 2" by 3" on a metal frame. It was noisy during the night—some trench mortar fire and occasional rifle grenades, and we had two men out on a listening post.

The sporadic mortar fire kept us dodging. Actually you can't dodge them. You are just as likely to run into them as to run away from them. Most Hun trench mortar had base fuses which show a thin trail of fire by night and a wisp of smoke by day. When they reached their zenith, these signs vanished as they turned over and over. Only the "chuck-chuck" of a falling object, increasing in speed and intensity, indicated their destination. The best protection was to flop in the bottom of the trench and pray that this one didn't have your number. Of course, the enemy gunners had a target and if you were sitting on that target, there wasn't much you could do about it. Hence we earned the sobriquet, P.B.I. (Poor Bloody Infantry).

The next six days was spent in reserve. Here we lived in the Cenot mine, an immense cave which could hold a couple of thousand, formerly a limestone quarry. It was almost a rest cure, entirely bomb-proof, with good water that the army managed to poison with bleaching powder. You could idle your days away in the shelter. At night, we had working parties, burying cables – telephone cables (radio and its adaptations had not been heard of) in preparation for the Vimy scrap. Returning to billet in the early morning, I had a slight mishap.

We were tired and walking rather slowly through a shallow trench back to the mine. We were probably seen, for a few shells came over and passed, but this quickened our steps. Then one exploded rather close. I didn't hear that one! A sliver of steel hit the back of my tin hat and knocked it off, bringing me to my knees. The chap behind helped me up but I said I was okay. I was shaken. I gingerly picked up the piece of metal for it was still warm. I carried it a piece. It was about nine or ten inches long and weighed about a pound. Too big for a souvenir so I tossed it away. The incident gave me a healthy respect for shell fire.

One day a "sausage" (minnie") dropped into my post but it was during my time off. One man was killed and three wounded. One of the wounded didn't seem to have much wrong but said he couldn't get up. Two of the boys carried him out but came back with the story that a whiz-bang came near and the wounded man jumped off the stretcher and got to the dressing station ahead of them. Maybe. He died in the dressing station.

The next trip was in the front line where I had the job of taking turns on the fire-step and watching through the darkness and barbed wire. The man who altered shift with me complained that he was unfairly treated for he was doing an extra trip. I immediately offered, and did, an extra shift to promote harmony. When he took my place, I went to the relative safety of the dugout. Shortly after that, the enemy tossed over three or four trench mortars. We climbed out to see if anyone was hurt. None, except this one man. He complained he was injured but was able to walk. Apparently shock. He was dead before morning. One taken and the other left! It had a sobering effect.

There were many of those six-day trips following the same pattern. I have lost track of their number. Some days were quiet and you were asleep on your feet. It seems natural that my first impressions were of what the enemy did to us. But it was routine that when the enemy tossed over trench mortars, our trench mortars and light field guns opened up. This soon became an artillery duel lasting by the hour. We were always happy to hear our guns start. But still, our attention was directed to what was coming at us.

I was again in the front line, alternating with staring over the top, staring into the darkness, when a raid by the enemy took place on our right. There was a lot of noise but we didn't know what was happening. A lad, standing beside me said,

"I hear someone talking Hun," dropped to his knees and emptied his rifle at an approaching shadow coming around the bay leading to our trench. It was all over in a minute. He said, "I got him!", and got up from his knees. Then he staggered against me saying, "I'm hit!" I dropped my rifle and put an arm around him, "Where?" "In the shoulder. He fired a revolver." I half led, half carried him up the trench. He straightened up and said, "I can make it to the dressing stations." Realizing I was unarmed (you don't drag a bayoneted rifle with you when you dodging for your life), I grabbed a Mill's grenade from a box near the dugout and crept back to regain my rifle and continue the watching vigil. It was later reported that our lads had captured a wounded soldier!

The next night, the artillery decided to give the enemy some punishment for the raid. We were ordered out of the front line, which would receive a pounding and took up positions midway between front line and support line. It had been a trench but was now a row of shell holes. Our guns opened up and pounded the enemy lines. The enemy, of course, expecting attack, pounded our front line.

We were in the unhappy position of collecting the shorts and overs of exploding shells. The punishment went on by the hour—both ways. Most of us could keep our heads below machine gun fire but there was no protection from shrapnel. Chunks of iron were flying in all directions. I know that one young soldier was surprised to find himself still in one piece when the lull finally came. I don't think I was really scared, but certainly kept my head down as far as the earth would let me. Someone was hit up our line and the call was passed along, "Stretcher bearer!" Then I met someone whose voice I knew—the Scottish burr. Tom was now a stretcher bearer. He paused, and asked, "Where?" I said, "Further up the line. Good luck to you."

PREPARATIONS FOR VIMY

We were relieved by the 20th Battalion at 2:00 a.m. next morning. After a series of short marches we ended up at Auchel (d'Auchel) on February 14 for three weeks' divisional rest. We went back to a training area out of the sound of guns. We went over the old infantry training, bayonet-fighting, and bomb throwing. (This was part of the re-grouping for the Vimy Ridge affair, but we did not know it then.)

At Auchel, life is a round of military drill in the mornings, lectures and demonstrations in the afternoons and church parade on Sundays. I guess I had time to think. It seemed a little frustrating. I had been some 19 days in the trenches, hadn't fired a shot in anger, and took what seemed like a lot of punishment. I'd been cold—it dropped to zero one night— hungry, lousy. Is this the way we fought a war? I am aware that my story so far sounds as if the infantry acted like a bunch of scared rabbits. So much for first impressions. But it was not always so. We were young and bounced back quickly.

During this period, we were introduced to the "model platoon" formation, or should I say, theory. It was demonstrated how the organized platoon could clear a trench of the enemy. The platoon was divided into four sections, bayonet men, rifle men, bombers and rifle grenadiers. The bayonet men went first, followed by the rifle men who fired over their heads. The bombers, in a bay behind, tossed their bombs over the leading men to clear the trench and the grenadiers came last and fired their Mill's bombs on nine inch rods to fall well in advance of the leaders.

On March 16 we were moved into support line on Neuville St. Vaast front. The time was spent as a working party at night digging trenches. Rumors were that we are to take

Vimy Ridge this spring. (I didn't know where Vimy Ridge was.) This was at the foot of Vimy Ridge, working in the tunnel which was later to play a part in that battle.

One night, I was one of a work party of eight men, carrying bags of chalk up the stairs and into the open for 50 yards or so. The tunnelers were working 24 hours a day in shifts, digging out the chalky limestone and putting it into sandbags. The night shift, us this time, carried the chalk away at night. That all sounds so simple. But the tunnel entrance was but a short distance behind the front line. Each man, in turn, would grab a bag, say 40 pounds, lug it up the stairs on his back and carry it some distance and spread it. It wouldn't do to have a ring of chalk around the tunnel entrance to give away its position. Although the enemy couldn't see him, the carrier was the target for any stray burst of machine gun fire or the odd trench mortar. It was an eerie job and hard work too. You were given a dirty job and you did it. But it just wasn't my cup of tea.

We were digging trenches by night and sleeping by day in the Cenot Mine—a huge underground quarry. There is a well at the mine entrance. The well is equipped with an endless spring lift. It is something to get a drink of water minus the gasoline flavor. The catch is that a guard at the well has orders to put a heaping teaspoonful of bleaching powder in each water-bottle. I wonder what is best for one's insides, gasoline or chlorine?

At night, we were relieved and marched out to Villers aux Bois and then to Bruay for a rest. We had a bath at Houdain. I had almost forgotten what a bath was like.

On March 30, we left Bruay for the line. For the first few days of April, we were in support line trenches on working parties both day and night. One of these was digging a trench to bury telephone cables. Our guns were pounding the ridge ceaselessly. It seemed quite safe to stand on the trench parapet in daylight and watch the shells exploding on the ridge. One of our platoon was killed when a loose driving band from one of our shells hit him on the back of the neck. The Huns made no reply by day.

Then it was out to Villers au Bois for 48-hour rest. We were told we would take Vimy Ridge on Sunday. (Perhaps an attempt at secrecy for attack commenced at dawn Monday.) We were to be in reserve 48 hours and in front line 48 hours.

The night before we moved into the line for the Vimy affair, an item on the notice board said, Holy Communion would be conducted in No 37 and 38 huts (Hut 37 – Protestant, Hut 38 – Catholic) at seven p.m. Nothing in my mind suggested that any religious rite would keep a man from harm. I think rather that my Methodist background persuaded me that it was the thing to do. I hunted out Hut 37 in the dark. Not fear and not religion sent me there. I think my attitude was "What the 'ell. Don't know what we are going into. Doesn't cost anything, anyway." With eight or nine others, I met in a candle-lit hut and took communion. Around midnight, we lined up, battle order, leaving great-coats and kit-bags behind, answered a roll-call, and moved into the "line." We were going where things were going to happen.

Placed in a platoon, then holding a front line post, I present a rugged time in and out of the trenches during the winter. Lousy, usually hungry, never comfortable, scared stiff of shell-fire, it was far from a happy existence. It is not popular to remember such things. But I should like this to be an honest tale.

I was among strangers. Our corporal's name was Clarke. There was a platoon sergeant, but I never did know his name. Others I knew only by nick-names. I have now forgotten the number of the platoon, but I was in "C" Company. Many things, however, I do remember.

I never saw a map and had only a vague idea as to where we were. For war news, we depended on rumor. For months, one of those rumors was that in the spring, we were going to "take" Vimy Ridge. The Ridge, however, was not a rumor. Looking over the front line trench at night, we looked slightly upward. It didn't seem much of a ridge, just a slope. We were all aware that the enemy was on higher ground. It was dangerous to move anywhere in the trenches in daylight. "He" could look right into most of our lines.

I have used an awful lot of words to give the background for the Battle of Vimy Ridge, an all Canadian victory, and the turning point of World War One. This was deliberate so that the reader would appreciate the preparation and the finality.

Around midnight, we were in the trenches.

VIMY

The story of the Battle of Vimy Ridge of April 9, 1917, Easter Monday, has been told many times. It is not the present intention to add to the story. This is merely to record how little the individual private soldier who took part knew about what was happening and the insignificant part he played.

Vimy! I had a grandstand seat!

After a stumbling night march, we shuffled in the darkness into a shallow trench. It was about three feet deep, and we sat there with orders to be ready to move at a moment's notice. Our platoon was placed in a trench just in front of the Lens-Arras road, behind most of the guns

There was a light rain. We draped our rubber sheets as capes, tucking our rifles under our arms to keep them dry. It was cold. Under our rubber sheets, we dozed and tried to sleep. But excitement and sleep don't mix.

Before dawn, the barrage opened up. Guns on all sides were firing. At first, there was quite a display ahead, bursting shells on the ridge and the occasional flare-up when enemy ammunition dump was hit. But dust and smoke soon blotted out everything but the thunder of the guns. The enemy threw some shells our way, but the only ones we noticed were those which went over our heads, exploding behind us.

Excitement took hold. We were anxious to get going. At a given signal, just before dawn, all hell broke loose, annihilating any possible opposition. At the first light, we saw streams of prisoners marching toward the cages behind us. Whatever the price, victory was in the air. Later, we knew that this was premature.

Finally we got orders to move.

Moving forward was not very exciting. We stumbled around shell holes, each man with a bag of bombs at his side. For some reason, now forgotten, I was a rifle grenadier, wearing a red patch on my shoulder. This meant that my bombs had nine-inch rods attached, to be fired from the rifle. I was used to these. They were merely Mills bombs adapted to the rifle. I knew that they would carry a maximum of 90 yards when the rifle was held, butt on the ground, at a 45 degree angle, fired, of course with a blank cartridge.

But the landscape was changed. What, a few hours before had been a no-man's land of trenches and barbed wire, was now an undulating stretch of gray drying mud from the night's rain. Trenches had pretty well disappeared. The whole was pock-marked by shell holes. There was some scattered fire from distant enemy reserve guns but a lull in our own gunfire. It looked as if the battle had been won and that we had no part in it.

Within sight on our left, the Pimple, that steep projection on the side of the ridge, was still in enemy hands. A continuous fire of smoke bombs kept this strong point out of action. The Pimple was taken from the rear a couple of days later. We passed walking wounded and some prisoners going the other way.

By noon, we were on our way with orders to hold the old Hun front line. That sounded simple, but there was no front line—just a row of shellholes. In a short time, we reached the old enemy front line—or rather the place where that line had been. We were told to hold this line, awaiting orders.

Above us, the boys were digging in along the crest of the ridge. We were spread out in a ragged line by sections, six or eight men and a corporal, to remain together. We were the support line. In our party were six men and a corporal.

There was retaliation by the enemy. A distant battery, firing our way, knew where their old line was and kept up an intermittent fire of howitzer shells, deadly if close. You soon knew when to dodge and when not. When the salvo (usually three) was coming for you, the roar was terrific, and you dropped into the nearest hole.

A salvo came our way. One lad, a few yards in advance, stood on a little mound. I saw him stoop as I dropped into a hole. When we got up, he was gone—literally blown to pieces. We wandered around in concentric circles, looking for pieces. We found bits of flesh, bone, and equipment, a pitiful pile of bits and pieces. We put them in a sandbag. The body seemed to have evaporated. While the corporal made a notation in his notebook, we dug a hole in the side of a trench and buried our late comrade. The corporal impressed me when he added a final touch. He found two bits of stick and bound them in the form of a cross and put it on the "grave" for all to see. We had all helped with dead and wounded before and had no strong emotional feelings. The misfortunes of war.

Within a matter of minutes, before we had recovered from the first shock, another lad was standing on the same mound. He had picked up a long-handled enemy shovel and exclaimed, "There's his bomb-bag burning! I'm going to throw some dirt on it." "Keep away!" shouted the corporal. But as he spoke, one bomb exploded and scattered the rest. The chap dropped—we ran to help, but he was past help. A tiny blue mark at the base of the forehead told the story. A tiny bit of steel had entered the brain. Death was instantaneous. It sounds like a nightmare, but I am telling it exactly as it happened. Some things you can't forget.

About sundown, we got orders to move. We supposed that this meant forward, but no, we moved back a bit and were to spend the night in the tunnel entrances, just behind an old Hun line. We got sandwiches and tea. Apparently, our platoon losses were only part of what was going on along the line, and no counter-attack could come before dawn. The tunnel, we all knew about. Construction had been going on all winter. We had worked at it at times. It was said that the engineers were working feverishly to connect our tunnel with the enemy tunnel, to bring up supplies and take back wounded on the light railway in the tunnel. We were not allowed inside but might spend most of the night on the stairs. Lying on the steps was not exactly restful.

And so, we nodded until dawn. Probably we got some rations then. I have forgotten. Nobody was much interested in eating. Everybody was thirsty. Excitement makes one dry and our water bottles were soon empty. Thirst can be a punishment in itself. Later in the day, we moved again. This time to the new front line. Next day, we continued to occupy the same line of shell holes.

On April 12, it was our turn to become the front line. We moved up the ridge in single file, around shell holes and took over the newly dug front line trench. As we went up the ridge, we passed the relieved troops coming out. Then we were in the front line, a winding trench some 50 to 100 yards from where the ridge dropped almost straight down. We had a few scouts out in front of the trench. This was known as the La Folie Farm Front. The trench was quiet. We were all surprised at the height we had attained. Looking over the trench, we could see for miles; there was flat land below.

In front, a little to our left, on a road leading away to the east, a mile or so away, was a farm house. There, an enemy battery was active, perhaps only one gun. This one unit kept firing light shells—whizbangs—in our direction. Almost all the shells burst in the trees that covered the ridge below us. The occasional "dud" went over our heads. Apparently, we had no guns in position to reach his enemy effort. We knew, too, that the enemy was entrenched at the base of the ridge, but the heavy growth of green prevented us from knowing where.

Late in the afternoon, it started to snow. Visibility was nil. Each man dug a hole in the side of the trench to get away from the weather. The advance posts could hold the line. Any movement from below would have brought a shower of bombs. I found a shovel and finally got a funk hole big enough to crawl into. Everything was wet with the heavily falling snow. It had been muddy before but was now worse. Covered with a rubber sheet and hugging my rifle to my chest, I tried to sleep. I suppose I did sleep but I awoke sometime during darkness, wet and cold, and paced the trench to keep warm. I was soon joined by others.

In the morning, I was on a ration party, going back a few hundred yards. We saw one of our field guns being skidded uphill, pulled by 20 or more men with ropes. The reason for lack of artillery support was clear. The snow had stopped but had turned the ridge into a sea of mud. Some guns were firing on our right and a muttering of gunfire came from behind us, probably from the Pimple, which was still holding out. Apart from the desultory fire from the farmhouse, our sector was quiet.

Now we were treated to a little drama, so fantastic that it seemed unreal. An artillery officer and signaler crossed our trench. The officer climbed to the crotch of a dead tree and looked over the terrain below through binoculars. The signaler sat at the base of the tree and talked to somebody with a lamp or heliograph. The officer gave some instructions and we watched the signals being flashed back. The officer dropped his hand quickly, the light flashed and immediately three guns fired. All three shells exploded behind our trench, sending a shower of debris over us.

The effect, momentarily, was like an earthquake. It was not funny to be practically sitting at the cannon's mouth. The signaler was pretty busy for a few minutes. Of course, we realized that the shells were intended for another destination but the elevation was too low to clear the crest of the Ridge.

When the guns fired again, we kept down until the shells roared over, then popped up to see what happened. The salvo of shells fell in the courtyard of the distant farmhouse, which for a few minutes was hidden in smoke. Then, the enemy, evidently thinking this was an attack, commenced firing into the trees below. We watched for the next salvo, expecting to see the farmhouse pounded. But the three shells this time burst at a crossroad, half a mile further east, a spot clearly marked by what was left of the usual rows of trees. Not understanding the strategy, we were disappointed. Minutes passed. The officer dropped his hand, the light flashed; simultaneously, three shells were on their way. This time, they seemed to land right on the farmhouse. The enemy gun ceased firing.

But this was not the end. We now saw a strange sight. There was no wind. The pall of white smoke drifted slowly over the farmhouse. Out of the smoke emerged a gun and caisson pulled by two or three horses which swerved at the gallop to the road and up the road to the east. We could see the crew running alongside, trying to gain footing on the rapidly moving vehicle. It was a tense few minutes—would they get away?

At the strategic moment, I saw the officer drop his hand. Three shells roared over. It was a photo-finish. Just as the galloping cavalcade reached the point where our guns had previously registered, the three shells overtook them. The smoke cleared. There was no movement. The officer, watching through binoculars, waved his hand: "Cease Fire!" We were so thrilled at the perfect co-ordination of our artillery battery that no one—certainly no one—stopped to consider that some of the real heroes of Vimy were lying at the crossroad, their shattered bodies amid the shards of war.

The sun was getting low on April 13 before we got the order to advance. Our trench was a few yards from the edge of a big drop. In contrast to the rest of the battlefield, the hillside was heavily wooded with small trees. With no detailed instructions, we were to attack the enemy entrenched at the foot of the Ridge. At a given signal, we climbed out of the trench and walked the short distance to the edge of the descent. Where our lot was to go down was not a hill but a cliff. We could see nothing ahead. Trees and brush, now in leaf, obscured our view. We stumbled down tortuous paths used for years by the enemy. It was still muddy and we had to move slowly, grasping branches and roots to keep from falling. We were loaded for big game. Each man had a bag of bombs. I had rifle grenades and a supply of blanks to fire. We went down slowly in twos and threes. This descent took several minutes.

I expected every moment to hear a machine gun open up. But that moment never came.

What we did not know until now, was that one or some of our guns had been placed in position on a promontory some distance to our right, perhaps half a mile away. A gun, probably a single field gun, had been hauled to the crest of the ridge placed in position to enfilade the Hun position. Anyway, as we were near the bottom of the hill, a gun commenced rapid fire right under our noses. There were shrapnel bursts only yards away. Before we reached the bottom, we were halted or we would have walked into our own fire. Praise the Lord! Those guys could shoot!

Apparently the Hun rear-guard saw us coming and decided to run for it. They were all out in the open when the gun on our right sent one shell after another in rapid succession into the fleeing Huns. As we advanced, there was a system of enemy trenches and a few enemy dead. To our left, about 100 yards away, was a pile of bodies, thrown together by the shrapnel. In front of us, was a very high railway embankment, curving from our left to the far right. There were some buildings, probably the town of Vimy. On our far left was an underpass of the embankment—the enemy's escape route. One man reached the underpass and died there. I saw him. The rest didn't get that far. It was slaughter. Sure, it was gruesome— it was war!

We quickly spread out and occupied the embankment. There was no life beyond it. We dug fire pits along the top and waited to see what would happen next. But the happenings were over. In the language of the troops, it was "tout fini."

We dug in along the embankment and spent the night there with neither sight nor sound of the enemy. We had taken one wounded prisoner, a Bavarian. When it got dark, the pile of dead, now behind us, continued to burn; ammunition, bombs and other inflammables flared up with a weird glow. It was natural for us not to allow anything to mark our position. A couple of us took shovels and went back to throw dirt over the blazing pyre. It was a quiet night on our front.

The 60th Battalion was credited with the capture of two villages: Chaudiere, Petit Vimy and the town of Vimy

And that is the saga of one man's experience at Vimy Ridge. An unvarnished account. We did what we were told to do, suffered casualties but took our objectives without having the opportunity to fire a shot in anger.

AFTER VIMY - 87TH BATTALION

Next day the 58th Battalion relieved us. We marched most of the night around shell holes, which were mostly filled with water, to reach Pile-on (Pylone) Shelters, an old support area. Dirty, weary and hungry, after the march over a greasy trail, I was still able to grin when I saw an old sign stuck on the side of a trench: "Pylone."

Then came a Sunday and we had a battalion parade—in compact order (no loud speakers, of course). The colonel addressed us at length. I've forgotten his name but he did have a slight French accent. He recounted the achievements of the 60th and then, almost in tears, informed us that the 60th was being broken up to reinforce the 87th battalion. After the parade, I marched with a small party to a rest camp near Guoy Servins to join a new battalion.

April 30, 1917

> *Today, I got transferred to the 87th Battalion Canadian Infantry Grenadier Guard of Montreal – the 60th Canadians is no more. We have to work hard, but we are decently fed, and as we have been starved for the last month, we appreciate it. We have some of our own officers and N.C.Os.*

Okay, so I was now in the 87th Battalion. I wasn't too happy. They fed us better than the 60th but they paraded every day including Sundays and had squad drill in the mornings and lectures in the afternoons. However, the second Sunday was my last with the 87th!

That Sunday afternoon, after the morning drill, my name was called and I joined with 14 others for a lecture. I realized that all wore the red patches of a rifle grenadier. A pleasant young officer led us away and we sat on the grass while he explained a new percussion bomb, one that didn't depend upon a four-second fuse but exploded when it hit. You put the rod in the barrel and then withdrew the safety pin and then fired. It would go 200 yards. You mustn't drop it or it would explode and blow your head off. He went over and over this warning. It didn't impress me for I felt I knew more about this grenade than he did. I was younger than the rest and had received instruction and had fired one at Valcartier. I had been interested when I first handled it. Sure, you had to be careful with all explosives.

We then went into some practice trenches. They were deep and there was a firing bay in the middle. First, we needed a target and then each man would fire a grenade. A rusty biscuit tin, a cube of about twenty inches was found. Two men were detailed to pace off 200 yards and set up the target. You could hardly see the tin at that distance. One by one, the men entered the bay with the sergeant, who gave final instructions and dashed out, evidently badly scared of the thing. When the rifle popped, all heads went up to see where that one landed. Some came close, but all fell to the right of the target. I digested that. "They're all going to the right." I had a glance at the Sergeant's list. In true army style, it was alphabetical. Praise the Lord, "Willans" came last—the first time my name ever gave me a break.

These boys were experienced in grenade firing. That meant they held the rifle at a 45-degree angle. I memorized that, "45-degree angle, all fire to the right." When my turn came, all had gone to the right of the can. The sergeant gave me some instructions I didn't hear; I was busy memorizing,

"45-degrees, all fell right". When the sergeant safely got away, I took my time. I set the rifle at a rigid forty-five degrees, aimed at the can, and deliberately shifted the rifle ten degrees left. I knew that the trigger pressure always pulled the rifle a little to the right.

Before the smoke cleared, someone screamed, "He blew up the can!" It was only a simple competition, but I wanted to win. When we broke off, the officer stopped me and took my name and number. He told me that tomorrow I was to report to the 11th Brigade Light Trench Mortar Battery. I asked a few questions and he explained, "They asked for a rifle grenadier." This was his way of choosing one. I thanked him and left, not sure if the result was good or bad for me!

The little incident of grenade practice earlier calls for comment. It was not an accident that I was successful although I had no idea at the moment where it would lead. I had fired the same grenade months before at Valcartier. It was regarded as something new by this particular group. The officer and sergeant were, frankly, afraid of the thing. Their nervousness was contagious. I felt a bit superior, for I could have told them how it was constructed and the safety features. I was not afraid and then it was an advantage to watch how the others acted. The biscuit tin was a two by two foot cube, but being rusty, was just a speck at 200 paces. It was a competition and I gave it all I had just to beat the other fellow.

11TH LIGHT TRENCH MORTAR BATTERY

On Monday, May 7, I reported to the 11th Light Trench Mortar Battery. I thought I was going on a course, perhaps to learn more about rifle grenades. I didn't know for a few days that my life in the infantry was over. I never went back. I almost loved the 87th the evening before. There was rice pudding for supper. I had almost forgotten that such things existed!

At the battery, the Sergeant Major took my name and number and told me to bunk in one of the huts. When I walked into the first hut I came to, nobody was interested. There was a card game in progress. After a few minutes, when I had found space to unload my gear, one older chap, French Canadian, spoke up. He asked, "What's your home town?" I said, "Ottawa." "I'm from Ottawa, too. I was manager of the Francais Theatre there. This is a good outfit. Keep your nose clean and you'll stay with us." That was my introduction to "Zippo."

I didn't have time to learn anything about trench mortars. Three days later, we were lined up to go into the line somewhere in the City of Lens at the north end of Vimy Ridge. Just as the battery was ready to leave, my name was called and I was told to report to the Quarter Master Sergeant at Carency, a few hundred yards away. I wasn't told anything except to go. I went. There were some remarks about a new man being given a bombproof job. I didn't like that and, as it turned out, the job wasn't exactly bombproof.

I reported to the Quarter Master Sergeant at Carency. Ralph was a decent soul and I asked what I was to do. He explained that I would sleep in the tent with him and Pete, the mailman. I would cook meals for three, and at night I would go up the line with a machinegun limber to deliver rations and mail to our battery headquarters. That's all! Cook three meals a day—and I was one hell of a cook—and be on the road most of the night. I soon learned, Ralph was easygoing but he was the boss.

DELIVERING MAIL

Cooking over a coke fire under a piece of tarp to shed the rain wasn't fun but I got good at it. I soon found that you couldn't boil water in an iron Dixie over coke. You got the water real hot and threw in extra tea—a poisonous brew. I had a heavy piece of iron that would fry bacon or what have you. When Pete brought back eggs, I "boiled" them in the tea water. It made the tea kind of black but my patrons weren't hard to please.

At about dusk, I left with the mule skinner with a double limber—a couple of two-wheeled boxes hooked together—at a walk since the road was too rough for anything faster. Fortunately, the skinner—same one every night—knew his way around. I guess the mules did too. But not me. I was all in the dark. We went a couple of miles up the Lens-Arras road and then into the sprawling city of Lens.

Sometimes these were quiet trips as far as the battery headquarters. But there was usually some shellfire. Sometimes, one area was being shelled and we waited until the noise abated and made a run for it. Ever try to make a mule run? At other times, we went right ahead and it was seldom as bad as it looked. But, I didn't like the job. There was tension on every trip.

Almost always, a few shells fell among the shattered houses and tossed bricks about, but nothing to worry about. A half mile through Lens was our headquarter billet. I unloaded our rations and mail. Our lads were watching and ran out to grab the ration bags; the Sergeant Major took the mail. I could wait for the driver to return in an hour or so or I could walk. I could travel faster than the mules and the road wasn't a healthy place to stick around. Most nights, I walked. Back at the tent at 11:30 pm, I just flopped down. I would awake upon hearing someone mention breakfast and hustle to bring the coke fire to life, make tea, fry bacon and deliver it on the three tin plates we had. Nothing to do until dinner! I often wondered how the army cook got his job. Now, I knew. "Some have greatness thrust upon them." At least, I didn't go hungry.

On May 25, my brother, Art, paid me a visit. He was an observer with the Air Force, stationed a couple of miles away at Camblin L'Abbe.

That was the routine for 12 days. Our outfit had a replacement crew and did two six-day trips in the line with the Stokes guns. When shelling got too rough, the skinner rode the off mule and with a goad he carried, got them to gallop. Then, I was hanging onto the rear limber with my legs in the air. It wasn't a hard life but it wasn't a lazy one. Nothing to do all day but cook meals. Ralph always managed to make sure we got the best of the rations before they went up the line. Occasionally, when there was a leg of beef in the rations, I fried steaks. Better than the stew the boys in the line would get. All in all, it was much better than life in the trenches.

The Battery moved into the Line on the evening of June 4. The headquarters was again at Angres. I was still on "rations." Now, each night, we went the same road but turned right at Lens, a half mile between shattered houses to a "sunken" road. I always thought of it as a sunken road because it had been pounded so much and shoveled out so many times that it was a trail between two piles of trash. It was always very dark. I never saw it in daylight.

We turned at Shrapnel Corner, a well-known spot where

a large camouflage net is hung across the lane by day and dropped at night. Usually we unhooked the rear limber and I stayed with it for half an hour or so while the driver was delivering his rations. There was a fairly solid bit of brick wall in front of the corner house. There was always some shellfire in the area and the wall gave a little protection. I spent several nights hugging that wall. I can't say I liked it but you do what you must do.

I soon found out why it was called "shrapnel corner." While I waited, a few shells came over, well ranged to sweep the corner. These were the "whiz-bangs" of the trenches that fire like a rifle, at almost the speed of sound. You heard the gun fire and the shell explode, almost as one. They were deadly if you were in front of them, spraying their load of steel balls always forward. Behind them, you were relatively safe. That first night, I crouched in a ditch, with a low garden wall of stone at my back and the half limber in front. If I wasn't exactly enjoying myself, I wasn't too worried. I had had experience with whiz-bangs before.

This became routine for ten of our twelve nightly trips. A few shells over the corner came most nights, but on the eleventh night, we were shaken out of this routine. I was down against the ditch as usual. I had an hour to wait. A high explosive shell, which sounded big, exploded down our sunken road. I got up and looked. There was nothing to be seen except the drifting smoke. A rising moon gave a little visibility. Another shell came in the same area. I knew the enemy was methodical in such things. I had a wrist watch, a cheap thing, but it kept going. I timed the shells—five minutes, then another. They continued five minutes apart until my driver appeared. I explained that it was worse to remain at the corner, which might become the next target. The driver agreed. I suggested, "Hook up the limber, wait for the next shell. Then make a run for it—we can make it in three."

The driver prodded the mules as they made the half-turn to our road. The chances looked good. But there was something I hadn't seen. A large camouflage net on two tall poles hung across the road by day. It had always been away before we came. This time, the net was coiled across the road like a huge snake. The mules refused to cross. The driver desperately prodded the mules. They leaped over the net, but a valuable minute was lost. It was a fast trip, me hanging behind with my legs in the air.

But this was our bad day. We got half way down the road and met a G.S. wagon coming toward us. The driver shouted, "I've got a load of ammunition and gotta get through." I had a momentary flash of a load of ammunition going up with "tout finis" for all. Minutes were wasted. We couldn't go back; the limbers would only go in a circle. Another shell came, landing somewhere behind the wagon. The horses bolted. But mules have more in their heads, and they don't like horses.

Amid the smoke and stink of high explosives, the mules dashed up the dirt pile while the G.S. wagon went away at a gallop. We circled back on the road. My feet seldom touched the ground, but I tripped over a body and heard someone yell. In another minute, we were in the shelter of the deep trench.

FINDING HELP FOR WOUNDED MAN

The ration party grabbed the rations and ran. I gave the sergeant major the mail and told him there was someone hurt down the road. Could I have someone to help? There was no helpful response. Most of the boys had their boots off, ready for bed. I was angry.

I went back up the road alone. There was a chap on the side of the road, quite conscious, pleading for help. I knelt beside him. There was nothing I could do in the dark. I couldn't even see where he was hit. It looked as if both legs were off. Perhaps they were just doubled under him. I ran back to the trench, at least two men could carry him. The muleskinner, of course, must remain with his mules, and was waiting for things to cool off.

I didn't know the way to the dugout but followed the trench until I came to a gas curtain, pulled it aside and climbed down. In the cellar were a number of our lads, partly undressed. I asked for someone to help. No volunteers. Then one corporal, whom I happened to know, said, "I'll come with you, Len."

I went back up the road and he followed on the verge above. We had just reached the wounded man when another shell came, some distance away. The corporal called, "I'm hit! Got a piece of shrapnel in my arm." He disappeared in a hurry. I didn't know what to do—I couldn't desert a man on the road.

I went back to the trench, passed the dugout—no use stopping there. Another gas curtain—I went down. Our officers were there. In any conversations with our O.C. (Officer Commanding), I found he was always reasonable, even kindly, although the boys all hated him. Now, I suppose he could see I was upset. When I explained, he said, "We're not equipped. You need a stretcher and a first-aid man. Go to the dressing station." "Where?" "Go up to shrapnel corner and turn left; it is not far. You'll see the Red Cross flag." I went.

When I got near the corner, another shell exploded in a nearby house. A man ran out and I followed him up the Angres road. I saw the flag and entered a cellar. The place reeked of antiseptic. While I waited a couple of minutes for the orderlies, I watched a surgeon taking a piece of shrapnel from a man's leg.

I went with the two orderlies with a cart and stretcher, and showed them where the wounded man lay. They definitely didn't want me around. I walked back to Carency. I've told a long story, but most was done at the lope and the time element was short.

The next day, a Non Commissioned Officer from the battery came out to arrange billets for the coming rest. He told me he passed three bodies, sewn in blankets on the side of the sunken road. The next trip with rations, the last before relief, was uneventful. I did notice that the bodies had been removed.

SUMMER ON THE LINE

On June 11, King George visited. I suppose you could call it a visit. We stood on the roadside and developed three cheers as the Royal Entourage went past.

A couple of days later, the battery came out of the line to rest for a few days and then went in reserve to Berthonval Woods. On June 30, they moved to Grand Servins for Divisional rest. I joined them there for training. Now the battery was out of the line for nearly a month. During that time, I was odd-job man. I went to the ration dump daily with Ralph and then carried the rations to the battery. We got a load of old lumber and Ralph and I built a shack to replace the tent which had seen better days. It was now summer but there had to be three meals a day. We didn't see much of Pete, the mailman. He had further to travel and delivered the mail himself.

On Divisional Rest during July, our time was spent in training. Half our training was in pursuit of the Model Platoon idea. I was in the rear rank with rifle grenades. We put on a show twice for different infantry units. We had empty bombs and grenades for this purpose and collected them after the demonstration. There was difficulty in obtaining blanks for the grenade firing, so that Jack-of-all-trades, the cook, made some. He simply pulled the bullet out with pliers. The blank could be then be filled with tallow and the case lightly crimped. He had no tallow so plugged the cartridge case with beef fat. The blanks looked all right and might have been so in the Arctic. But in the hot July sun, the fat got soft. I had one misfire. The cap went off and merely blew the cordite into the rifle barrel. The grenade fell a few feet in front of me. We had been told that we would soon be inspected by General Currie and would put on a show using live bombs and live grenades. After the practice, I told the C.S.M. about the blanks, but he had other troubles and refused to listen.

On July 19, we were inspected by General Currie and his staff of about 15 brass hats. After inspection, we put on our show, which was to capture a line of trenches in Model Platoon style. The rifle grenadiers, four of us, had been issued with the cook's blank cartridges. At a signal, we were to fire live grenades over the heads of our comrades. I was very unhappy. Frankly, I was scared stiff. But the army training creates a robot mentality that makes a man do asinine things if he is ordered to do so. The man next to me fired so I fired one. Both grenades sailed well over the target. (The Mill's Grenade would go 90 yards and had a five-second fuse, which would give it a graze burst at that distance.)

We each had six bombs and had to fire fast to get them all away before the cease fire. I dropped again on one knee, pulled the pin of my second grenade and pressed the trigger. "Pop!" Only the cap fired; the grenade slipped out of the steel retaining cup and then slipped back, the fuse sizzling. I had an activated grenade at the end of my rifle with a scant five seconds to go!

I did the only thing I could do. I wheeled about, yelled, and ran back, counting one, two, three. Then I threw rifle, bayonet and grenade as far as I could. I went down with my nose in the grass roots wondering if a tin hat would stop shrapnel. As I went down, I saw the grenade slip out of the rifle and roll another foot or so, with a trail of smoke. I also saw, and this was a surprise, that the inspecting officers were following us. However, some must have seen and appeared to be edging away. Waiting for that blessed thing to go off was the longest few seconds I had ever known. When the big bang came, within a measured distance from my head, I grabbed my rifle and rejoined the line, but by now the show was over.

Three of our boys picked up some shrapnel in that affair. One went to hospital. When we marched back to billets, I noticed blood on my rifle. Then I found that blood was running down my arm and dripping from my fingers. I pulled off my tunic and there seemed to be blood everywhere. I looked for a shoulder wound. Not until I washed off the blood did I find that a bit of shrapnel had sliced across the knuckles of my left hand. As we had been carrying rifles at the "high port," the blood had run up my arm. As it wasn't popular in our battery to say anything about what had happened, I tied a rag around my hand until it stopped bleeding. We didn't put on any more shows with "live" grenades.

It was a comparatively easy time for me. Then, on a few hours' notice, the battery was back in the line, again on the Lens front with our headquarters in the same place as when I first started the ration job. I was again staying at the Carency mule lines to deliver rations to Battery H.Q. in Lievins, part of Lens city. The Battery was in for a rather long trip, until the middle of August.

One day, a lone Hun plane dived out of the clouds near Carency and shot down one of our observation balloons. A.A. batteries opened up and the observer came down via parachute. The Hun dived after the parachute with guns streaking. One of our planes dived out of the clouds and shot down the Hun, a four-minute drama.

At the end of the first week of August, my driver was slightly wounded. One of the mules got a piece of iron in his dinner basket. He limped home, but there was no first aid for mules. Of course, it had to be shot. I was present at the execution, which nearly broke the mule skinner's heart. I was grieved too.

Each nightly trip with rations was an event. Perhaps there was more noise than actual danger. A shell exploding among the shattered houses lining both sides of the road on the outskirts of Lens makes a big racket and throws about bricks and debris. Let's say it was unpleasant in the dark.

The trips were routine: the same occasional shelling and the usual gallop to get away from them. But one night, it was different. A salvo of gas shells came over and exploded beside the road. I recognized their buzzing sound and knew they were supposed to contain the Hun's yellow cross gas, said to be lethal. They weren't lethal, or I shouldn't be writing this. There were three, I believe, in the salvo. The mules galloped, but I didn't. I was immersed in a cloud of poison gas. I staggered around with my respirator in my hand, unable to get it on. I knew there was an artillery battery somewhere close. I ran against a roadside wall. I found a gas curtain and tangled with it, then collapsed and tumbled down some steps.

The boys there let me lie for a few minutes; they had heard the shells. Then, the one in charge, said, "You get up and go to the dressing station. They'll give you something there. Know where it is?" I nodded, couldn't speak. The dressing station was half a mile away. I went. I thought I was running but I guess it wasn't much of a run. I could breathe only with difficulty. I finally got there.

As I entered, the boys knew what it was and in a minute I was given a cotton-covered glass tube and told to "chew it." I took it gingerly, wondering what the glass would do to my insides, but was told the cover would absorb the glass. I chewed it. The sharp fumes of ammonia choked me, but what a blessed relief! They kept me there a while and gave me another tube, saying, "Chew that if it gets worse, or chew it in the morning. Come back if it doesn't work. Now, go and get some sleep. Have you got a place to go?" I nodded and left. I went the couple of hundred yards to our headquarters and bumped into our sergeant major, told him, then flopped on a blanket and went to sleep. Next morning, I conscientiously chewed the other vial, got a tin of tea and walked back to Carency.

I didn't make breakfast next morning, but by noon was ambling around. I suffered from recurring attacks of bronchitis for weeks after. I even got as far as a doctor and got a bottle of dope to take. That night, I went again with

the rations as usual although not exactly happy about
it. This was August. I had held my "bomb-proof" job since
the previous April. I was willing to trade jobs with anyone.
Through a change in ration arrangements, my job ended in
September.

The battery was back in the line, this time on the Merricourt front—an advance over the flat land below the ridge. I carried rations on my back, on a rough road across the flats below. It was a long trip and exhausting. I thought I could improve on it. I borrowed the mailman's bike and, with ration bags slung on it, pushed the load in the darkness. Fine! I thought I could ride back but the road was too rough for bike. After threatening to break my neck a couple of times, I walked and dragged the bike along. . It took all night.

The battery came out of the line to Chateau de la Haie soon after that and I continued carrying rations on my back now—no more mules—to various points where the battery was located. During this rest period I was a few days with the battery, got to know the boys and had some experience with the Stokes gun, firing blank shells on a range. Then I marched in a model platoon where I was again a rifle grenadier. We fired live bombs in this practice and I was always worried, for in case of error, we might kill someone. On one of these days, two of our boys got bits of shrapnel and one went to the hospital. During this period, I met Old Hitch. Hitch didn't have a friend and adopted me. He was 50 and looked after my interest. I reciprocated by being intensely loyal to him.

On September 19, after a few days out of the line, the battery switched to a new front: Avion, between Vimy Ridge and Lens. My ration job was over. A light railway brought up rations and ammunition. Without battle experience with the guns, I had various jobs. At first, it was on carrying parties to take ammunition up the line at night. The load was six shells, 60 pounds in two sandbags, from the railhead dump to the different gun positions. It was a relatively quiet front. When a few shells came our way, we crouched in a trench and hoped for the best. That job lasted a week.

Next, I was used as a runner to carry messages to the gun crews; at night, I was to learn the way so as to guide in another gun crew. The crew had a small dugout captured from the Huns, its doorway facing the enemy. It was a poor, exposed position. You could only get around at night. In daylight, you had to crawl in a shallow trench on a side-hill.

Early on in this job, I had to guide one of the officers up the line to inspect the gun positions. I hadn't had the time to really memorize routes and overland trails. The officer was more worried than I, for he had to depend on my knowledge of the route taken, but we made it without any problems.

My last tour of duty was an ill-fated expedition. I had to guide a gun crew to a new position chosen by map. The crew was to dig a gun emplacement and set up their gun. After guiding them, I was to return to headquarters, about an hour's walk through the trenches. We all got there without mishap. As our party arrived, the Huns started sending over minnies. We had to scramble for cover. The only place was the dugout where I had left five men the night before.

These boys were cooking supper over a charcoal brazier. There was no room inside so we sat on the stairs. It was one of those bad times. A minnie dropped at the doorway. I found myself on the dugout floor but my mind was working fast. I had been in a similar situation before and ever since carried a stub of a candle. I lit it but couldn't see for the thick smoke. I thought the rest were all dead and said, "Anyone here alive?"

We were 11 men altogether. Only three were able to move. We started digging with our hands. It seemed a long time before we made progress. Then we got a hole through to the outside and the smoke lessened. We got infantry to help us carry those who couldn't walk. Six went to hospital; one died. Of course, we all suffered from shock.

In the early dawn, I led the walking wounded back to the battery, a mental wreck myself. Old Hitch was one of the stretcher cases but a week in field hospital fixed him up. The Stokes gun we brought was gone and never seen again. Officially, it was destroyed by enemy action.

In late September, I went up the line with a gun crew. I had the satisfaction of sending over a few Stokes shells and felt a little happier to be able to hit back. One day, we fired a few shells over but apparently we were under direct observation. Each time we fired the gun we drew a lot of shell fire. We had a shallow bit of trench and two guns in shell-holes. At night, we would fire four or five rounds and then hike for cover. But there wasn't much cover. We had no dugout, just a funk-hole in the side of a trench. During this time, I got word that brother Art had been wounded with a machine bullet through his left hand and was back in Blighty. We got some re-enforcements from the infantry because we lost eight men in eight days in the Line. As our battery strength, on paper, was about 60, and our actual strength was closer to 40, our losses were high.

Then October came and the sky changed. Early in the month, we marched to Houdain. On the march, we had six "apple-carts" to hold the guns and baggage. With one man on the handles and four or five on the ropes, we rattled along, a most un-military-looking military unit.

Now came the day when we loaded our carts and commenced a long march, all day with a break at noon. This march went on for days. At one point, on a little hill at a crossroads called "The Four Winds," we were halted. We could see half a mile away an artificial hill, a huge mound. We were told that the mound had been erected to mark the site of the Battle of Waterloo. Could be. I hadn't the least notion where we were or where we were going. We were told that it was a "Corps Rest"; the whole Canadian Corps was on the move.

We did working parties in Ypres for a couple of days, mainly removing debris from cellars to make them useful for troops. Ypres, a contested area for so long was mostly a mass of rubble, with a few good cellars. Then we left Ypres for Poperinge on October 22.

We were back in Ypres on October 28th. The next day, I was on a burial party with the corporal and six others. Ed was given a map location and told to search the area for bodies that might have been missed. We did our job thoroughly, wandering around shell holes and mud, but found no dead. Finally, we stopped on a little mound to decide what to do. Before we had time to come to any conclusion, fate intervened.

We were on the return journey when a couple of shells exploded about a quarter of a mile away. One burst on contact and we heard the whirr of a chunk of iron coming our way. The corporal received it on his tin hat which went flying across the mud. When he retrieved his lid, it had a jagged hole of two fingers breadth – a souvenir and a headache. Otherwise, no harm done.

That ended the search.

We went back to the Menin road and reported at the White Chateau, a pile of rubble with one wall still standing. In the shelter of the wall, a long trench had been dug, with a row of bodies covered with a Union Jack. We stood at attention with doffed headgear while the padre read the brief burial service, a military funeral that left its mark. One would have been a clod not to have found the simple service impressive. Oddly enough, this was the only time I had been present at a military funeral!

We left the rest to the grave-diggers and marched back to Ypres. At that time, by the way, the old city moat, a relic of medieval times, still held water. On the sheltered side of the city (west), there were even some ducks paddling about!

PASSCHENDAELE

The Third Battle of Ypres, usually referred to as the Battle of Passchendaele, was not by any stretch of the imagination, a glorious victory. The battle for Passchendaele Ridge went on from July to the beginning of November, 1917. It was later said that the advance of five miles from Ypres to the Ridge cost the British 400,000 men. The brief but probably important part taken by the Canadians was an interlude between the fighting around Lens and Merricourt, in the vicinity of Vimy Ridge. The only excuse I have for telling this part of the story is that I was there.

I must explain briefly that I had received a sort of promotion. I was no longer just a private in the infantry. I was a Stokes Gunner. A member of the Light Trench Mortar Battery.

My transfer to a trench mortar battery was a big change in my army life. I joined a team, got to know the boys, found friends and got a chance to hit back at the enemy. Unconcerned about the right or wrong of the issues that caused the war, we were fighting for our lives and the freedom of those we had left behind. I got a grim satisfaction out of firing Stokes shells into the enemy trenches.

The Stokes gun was a rapid fire trench mortar. When conditions did not permit us to be of use, as trench artillery, we were odd-job men. We had a strength of around 40 men, commanded by a captain with a couple of lieutenants as aides. On the road we didn't march like infantry. We had a number of high-wheeled carts which held our guns and extra baggage, so we travelled light. One man held the cart handles and a half dozen more pulled on a rope. We lacked much military discipline but on the other hand, we worked as a team and the individual accepted more responsibility than the average infantry man.

A word about the Stokes gun. It was a war-time invention, a rapid trench mortar, with a range of half to three-quarters of a mile. The barrel was like a piece of gas pipe; the shell was a three-inch, ten-pound missile, and quite destructive. To fire, you pulled the safety pin and dropped the shell in the barrel. It slid down and hit the striking pin, and "pop" it was on its way. If need arose, you could fire as quickly as you could pull pins and drop them in the barrel, keeping three or four shells in the air at once. You couldn't really hit anything but you could cause a lot of grief at the receiving end. There were two types, one with a ten-second fuse and the other with an instantaneous fuse which exploded on contact.

The shells came into the line without fuses and detonators, for safety in handling. One little job was to insert the fuses and detonators. It was a bit tricky, for the detonators were slim copper tubes with attached fuses. The active principle was a delicate explosive, a fulminate of mercury. You handled them carefully. The detonator was likely to explode if you tapped it on metal or anything hard. One of our lads lost two fingers that way.

I did my share of preparing shells and didn't mind it. I worked out a system. Discarding equipment and rifle to get metal away from me, sitting on the trench floor with a pile of shells and a box of detonators, I was happy enough. I used a slim stick, usually a bit of willow, to clean out the detonator well in case there was a grain of sand or other obstruction in the shell. Then, it was nothing to slide the detonator into place and screw down the top. One more shell was ready. Of course I knew I mustn't make a mistake. If I did, the finale would be so sudden I wouldn't know anything about it.

Being with the trench mortars, I was spared a lot of the misery of trench warfare. But we were a suicide outfit losses were high.

We came out of the line about the end of September 1917. It was said we were going out for a rest. Rumour had it that we were going to Belgium. By slow stages, we did go there.

October saw us moving first by train—flat-cars—to Thiene, then back on the road marching to Ste. Marie Cappel. A few days' halt. Then at 3:30 in the morning of October 26, we did a forced march in light order—no guns or carts—during the hours of darkness. Everything was done in quick time. We entered the ruins of Ypres at the south-west corner, ate breakfast and immediately left Ypres through the Menin Gate on the east side. It was open warfare with no use for trench mortars so we were now stretcher-bearers.

Leaving Ypres, in front of us was nothing but an expanse of weird desolation. There was the one road—the Menin Road—and the view in every direction was a mess of mud and shell holes. Only one building was in sight, the White Chateau, what was left of a stone building at what had been a crossroad, a mile or so away. It was a flat but slightly rolling land, a muddy mixture stretching to the skyline. A few shells from long-range guns passed over into Ypres to remind us that the war was not so far away.

Our officers, baggage, some N.C.O.s and other personnel were left behind. We were about 30 men with a couple of N.C.O.s. Marching in double file up the road, dodging dump trucks, repairing the road constantly, and ambulances going up empty and coming back loaded, we got as far as the White Chateau.

This was a sort of jumping-off place for the stretcher bearers. From there, the road was subject to a desultory shell fire. We went another mile or so in small parties, dodging traffic until we came to the end of the road. Here, in a captured cement pill-box, was the dressing station where the ambulances picked up their load.

The "pill-boxes" were enemy gun emplacements, solid cement, six feet above ground and about the same below with only a machine gun slit facing our direction and a door below ground level behind. Most of them, which dotted the landscape at strategic points, were made to hold about six men, a sort of above-ground dugout. This one we reached was somewhat larger and had three rooms. It was occupied by doctors and medical orderlies and the waiting wounded.

Stretching ahead toward the front line was an apparently endless, winding trail of "duck-mats." These were 16-foot two-by-fours carrying cross slate which made travelling through the mud possible. Here and there, a "lucky" shell had blown up the duck-mat and made getting past quite a performance. Our job was to follow the duck-mats to the end and bring back wounded. The trail was anywhere between a mile and two miles, but it seemed to grow longer each time it was travelled. You shouldered an empty stretcher and were on your way.

At about half-way, you passed another pill-box with a Red Cross flag where you stopped on the return trip with each wounded man. The medicos checked him, applied new bandages where needed and a hypo, perhaps. Then you were waved on your way. At the end of the trail was another pill-box where the wounded were brought in. Here you got your load. On each trip, you ran into shellfire but soon learned to disregard it. There was so much mud and water that shells did not detonate on contact, but buried deep and then exploded, sending up a geyser of mud. Of course, if one was coming right for you, you flopped on the duck-mat and then got up rather surprised to find that you were still in one piece.

At your destination, you joined some other lads sitting in the lee of the pill-box and awaited orders. You found that it required six men to carry one out, one at each handle of the stretcher and two spare men for relief. Under those conditions, the weight on one arm soon became unbearable. When another wounded was released by the doctor, six men broke away and grabbed the stretcher. Pretty soon, you had lost your former companions, and all were strangers. But there was no slacking; each took his turn. It was better to be moving than waiting.

How many trips I made over those duck-mats, I now have no idea. I know it was a steady trek. The attack to take Passchendaele Ridge was on and there was plenty of work for us. I was carrying stretchers all that day and all night. On October 29 and 30, I worked 30 hours without food; every time I came down with loaded stretcher, I got a shot of rum.

The pattern was always the same. We stopped at the half-way house, had dressings adjusted and went on to where the ambulances came. Once our load was delivered, the medical officer would dole out a generous shot of rum and say, "Grab a stretcher and get back up there." We usually went back in pairs, a smaller target than six.

On one trip, I helped carry out a young officer. He was bleeding badly; in fact, the stretcher was becoming soaked with blood. He was quite conscious. We carried on a conversation most of the way. He told me that he had just returned from Blighty, had just received his commission and this was his first trip in the line since his return. I tried to give some word of comfort—that we would soon get him where he would get help, but I knew he couldn't last long. We stopped half-way, but the medical officer shook his head and waved us on. He died before we reached the end of the journey and we loaded him directly on the ambulance.

When things were at a height, in the late afternoon, we caught up with other stretcher parties at the half-way point. There were six or seven stretchers in a row, each with their six bearers, the whole moving slowly like a long snake down the duck-mats. An enemy plane came over, circled to get the sun at his back and returned to shoot us up with his machine guns. Some of the boys had Red Cross flags which they waved frantically. But there was no gallantry in this war. Down went the stretchers and we lay in the mud. Machine gun bullets "sputted" on all sides. We seemed immune. No one was hit. We got up and went on. The plane again circled and came at us a bit lower with its two synchronized guns firing. Again, we flattened out. Again, no one was hit. That was that.

Late in the day, but still light enough to see, with a few others I lay crouched against the lee side of the forward pill-box. It was one of those brief rests. The pill-boxes were, of course, enemy targets and got a fair share of the shellfire.

A few yards away, in a shallow trench full of mud and water, a small party of Aussies, about ten, came slowly splashing along. We were interested, for we recognized them by their distortion of English and wondered what they were doing here. This is the only humorous incident that I recall during the grim episode. Perhaps it wasn't funny. Some shells, with their usual roar, announced their arrival. We froze to the ground. One shell seemed to explode right in the water filled trench. Before the smoke drifted away, the trench had the appearance of a wading pool.

We heard the Auzzies counting heads. Then "Are you all right, Diggah?" "Where's Diggah?" By this time, we were on our feet to help dig out Diggah. But Diggah was bent on survival. Something resembling a prehistoric monster arose from the ooze. After his complete immersion in a mud bath, Diggah did a lot of blowing and snorting. The figure was so encased in slime that it was some minutes before Diggah could express what he thought of the enemy. Then we heard a marvelous string of new oaths. Diggah was reasserting his dignity.

One time, I was carrying an empty stretcher back to the forward area when one of our corporals caught up with me.

He was taking a message up the line. There were quite a lot of howitzer shells coming over. We ignored them as a rule, for they buried in the soupy soil and exploded when they hit something hard, sending up geysers of mud.

This time, my luck seemed to have run out. We had reached a spot where the trench mat had been blown up and were picking our way through the mud, when a salvo came over. We heard the shells roaring and apparently coming right for us. The messenger was a little ahead and started to run. I just dropped. One of these babies landed a few feet from me and burrowed in the mud. I got a complete mud bath. I got to my knees, choking from the acrid smoke. He couldn't see me for smoke but came back to pick up the remains, I suppose. He was startled to see me getting up and exploded, "That one sure fanned your ass, Len!" A little thing like that leaves a scar on your memory!

It was a long afternoon, a long night and a long day. On one occasion, four of us were lying behind the forward dressing stations, a cement "pill-box." The cement wall, two feet above ground, gave some protection. But the pill-box was an enemy target.

The second day, one trip ended in tragedy. I was with a stretcher party. It took eight men to carry one out, six on the stretcher and two for relief. We were moving slowly along, taking turns on the stretcher when an old friend caught up with us—Zippo, who was first to welcome me when I came from the 87 Battalion. In his usual style, Zippo said, "I'm on my way out. I'm going to find billets for you'se guys. You'll be relieved in a couple of days." He didn't fulfill that ambition. When we reached the Menin road ambulance station, a few shells came over and Zippo received a head wound. We put him in the waiting ambulance. We were depressed to hear, a week later, that he had died in hospital. Zippo was the most popular lad in the battery.

During the night, the stretcher parties continued, but slower. In many places, we just stumbled along. The shots of rum were fewer and seemed to have lost their potency. There were more rest periods but no sleep. When the sun came up, we were looking for a relief party which failed to materialize. We went on.

Some time in the morning, I reached the limit of endurance. More than 24 more hours without food or sleep, travelling on odd shots of rum. The human animal can stand just so much. Perhaps it was the last shot of rum. I don't know. I think I was just looking for a place to lie down and sleep. I got on the road headed toward Ypres.

I met another lad. "Where are you going?" "To Ypres and breakfast." He joined me. One after another, I picked up a following. Then a familiar face appeared, Old Hitch. "Where are you going, Len?" "To Ypres." He joined my little army. By the time we passed the White Chateau, I had a party of between 20 and 30. Here was me, a glorified private leading a marching column and enjoying it.

After we passed the Cloth Hall in Ypres, I saw a Red Cross flag, halted my squad and went down a few steps into a cellar to investigate. I told the medical officer, who was sitting at a table, that I had a party of men who hadn't eaten for 24 hours. He was a kindly soul and as all his visitors were equally mud-splattered, he probably thought I was an officer. "Take your men to the kitchen," he said, explaining where an emergency kitchen had been set up. "When they are fed, bring them back and I'll give them a shot of rum." I thanked him and dutifully carried out orders.

We had a wonderful meal, hot baked beans, bread, butter and tea—with second helpings! After that, I had no difficulty in persuading "my men" to pay a return visit to the medical officer. When I reported back, he said, "Tell your party to come down in single file," and poured out a generous shot of rum for me. I accepted gratefully. Then he said, "Stay with me and count your men, so I'll know when they are all served." I tried, but issue rum, before it has been watered, is potent stuff. To count was beyond me. I didn't even know any of the faces. I knew some were doubling up in the line and it worried me. When I saw Old Hitch appear for a second time, I said, "The last man, sir." I thanked him for his help but he said, "Wait a minute." He poured me another drink. I didn't really want it but he had been so decent that I felt it would be churlish to refuse.

Next act in this rather childish drama, Old Hitch and I stood arms around each other, holding each other up, on the edge of the road we had to cross to reach our billet, the Armory. We were afraid to cross because of the traffic. Once we found our bunks of chicken wire, removed boots and rolled into muddy blankets, we slept the clock around. This was late in the afternoon. I had worked for some 30 hours without respite, had been through a little bit of Hell, and was drunk for the only time in my life.

We were billeted at the time in a convent. We left Ypres by train, later by trucks, back to France on November 19. The Canadian Corps was out for a long rest—to lick their wounds, for the Passchendaele trip had been mighty expensive. We were away from the line most of the rest of November and into December, marching to various small towns: Merville, Ourton near Bruay and camps in between.

LEAVE TO ENGLAND

I got a break I had never dreamed of. I had been almost a year in France and received fourteen days leave to "Blighty." On December 12, I was sent to the paymaster who emptied my paybook, paying me 15 pounds and 25 francs for the trip. I entrained at Coulogne-Riquart and went from Boulogne to Folkstone.

In the process, I got a replacement for my blood soaked tunic but was told to scrape the mud from the rest of my uniform. I managed to see Art in the evening. He was an out-patient at the Prince of Wales Hospital. The next day I spent in London with Art. I also visited Winnie Harris, Ollie's cousin in Lewisham, then left at night for a visit to our cousins at West Hartlepool. I managed a day in Leeds to visit family.

On December 26, I left West Hartlepool for London and France. As the hour of departure was very early, I insisted on going to the station alone. I wasn't afraid to go back but I guess I can admit there were other places I would rather be than on my way to France. On the station platform, I ran into another in the same boat except that he was a little tight and had a bottle of rum. I took a drink to pacify him and lost him getting on the crowded train. The train was loaded with lads going back. I stood most of the way to Kings Cross and most of the night!

Back in France on December 27, I had to find our battery. Except that they were in the line, nobody could tell me where they were. I walked and hitch-hiked all day, still enquiring and found our headquarters in the evening. I had a couple of days' rest and was then in the line with the guns. This was a two-man crew, a corporal and I, on the Merricourt front.

Actually, our forces held Vimy and the enemy Merricourt. Obviously, the line here had not advanced much since the Battle of Vimy Ridge. There were miles of flat land which was a network of trenches. It was difficult to know which were ours and which were held by the enemy. What we regarded as our front line was 2000 yards from the enemy line.

By day, the two of us lived in a crude shelter, a piece of sheet iron over a hole in the side of the front line. At dark, we walked a long way, over a quarter mile. There, with an infantry screen in front of us, from a deep trench behind a mound was our gun and shells. We would fire a few shells and run for cover to dodge the reply which came in the form of a few whiz-bangs. We repeated this all night, then went back to our tin shelter.

In early January, our front line was about a thousand yards from the enemy but in the evening, our crew moved forward through a maze of old trenches until we were within range of the Hun line. We fired 40 or 50 rounds from each of two guns aimed at the Hun front line and his wire. The enemy replied with quite a lot of shellfire but it went away over our heads. He was not using trench mortars. We had an infantry screen in front. During the day, we rested in a funk-hole, in what was the actual front line. Except for a few whiz-bangs, we had a quiet six-day trip. This whole program looked like a waste of ammunition. We probably didn't do much damage. Of course, 80 to 100 rounds of Stokes shells along his front line every night kept things stirred up. This was a nightly exercise for six nights. There was, of course, plenty of artillery exchange between both sides.

We were of the line for six days, carrying shells up to the line and acting as runners. It wasn't exactly quiet in Lievins. The Huns were sending over big air-burst "Woolly Bears" that made a lot of smoke and noise and had some iron in them. Our ammunition job consisted of bagging shells at a rail-head ammunition dump (an unhealthy place during shellfire) by day and carrying it up the trenches at night, six ten-pound shells per man. I would have traded this job for any I've ever had. A few shells fell around the ammunition dump while we were working there. In the evening, we used a light railway for the first part of our trip. A Hun shell made a direct hit on the railway and made a mess of it, causing seven infantry casualties. From then on, we had to tote our bags of ammunition that much further.

SACRIFICE GUN PLACEMENT

The next six-day trip was, at least, unusual. Someone higher up got the bright idea of a sacrifice gun on a front where an attack was expected. Jack, an older man and a good soul, and I were elected to be the crew. This was another sector of the Merricourt front, the side of a "wedge" where an attack might come. The attack didn't materialize, or I shouldn't be now telling about it.

All Jack and I had to do was crawl in the darkness of the early morn along a narrow "sap" (slit trench) under our barbed wire and set up the gun in a deep shell crater, 75 yards in front of the front line. (There was a well-organized front line at this point.) There we lay all day until darkness allowed us out, back to a funk-hole in the front line. The only instructions we had were, "In case of attack, fire the gun while you can then use your rifles."

Both Jack and I knew it was a crazy scheme. The first barrage fire would eliminate us before we had time to fire the gun or do anything. But we were old soldiers and obeyed orders. For the six days, we did our stuff. I have known better days! Finally, we got so bored, we almost wished something would happen.

After this trip, the battery had a brief rest. Around this time, I had a short talk with Captain Black. I told him I had a brother in the Flying Corps and would like to join him. Captain Black wasn't enthusiastic but said he would look into it. "You might have a chance." This was January. It was May before I heard any more about it.

Then it was on to Bruay. Nearly everyone in this town worked in the mines There were rows and rows of small brick houses. Because Hitch and I were "friends," we were billeted together in one house—two men to a house down the row. It was a real home—man, wife and three children and apparently Hitch and I had a bed together. Of course, we gave what little we had to the wife. The family was paid for room but didn't have to supply a bed.

We lasted there about ten days. The oldest child, a girl about 15, Madlon (I became Lee-o-nar), had a crush on me right away. I became an artful dodger. She borrowed a bottle of scent and a tin of talcum from my kit—don't remember where I got them. She pestered me to take her to the "ceenema!" I hadn't the money and couldn't see myself acting as escort to watch an old rerun in French! She insisted on teaching me French. The two younger children, twins, a girl and a boy were named (in English) Jean and Jeanne. To me, they were "Zhon et Zhon." A gale of laughter followed my attempts. I still can't distinguish between the two names.

Our upstairs window looked down upon a row of identical small courtyards. For the miner, Sunday was bath day. It was amusing to look down on a Sunday morning at the wooden tubs in the middle of each little yard, the male members in the tubs and the distaff half scrubbing their backs. La Belle France!

UP THE LINE AGAIN

In the first part of March, we marched to Carency with all our junk and then went "Up the Line."

March 12, 1917

Last night, we slept in "The Chateau" at Guay-Servins, a place worthy of mention. It was the biggest house I ever slept in. We put a whole battalion—900 men—in it. It was "U" shaped and with its outbuildings enclosed a huge courtyard. It was owned by people called "Servins" who became bankrupt; then the building was taken over by the French government. There were two watch-towers, one on either side of the big iron gates. The whole structure was stone but was falling to pieces.

Lens had been taken street by street and the enemy was now forced into the suburbs. It was a really large city, all coal mines, loading tipples and underground tunnels. We had several casualties while in Lens. A gun crew of three had one gun and a deep dugout that ended in a tunnel. Something happened—nobody knew what—and the "dugout" blew up. One of the crew was with the gun at the time; although injured, he came back to report. An attempt was made to dig the other two out. But there were tons of rock in the hole and the place was under observation. Finally they were reported "killed in action."

I did two trips with the guns, once with an older man. He was not so spry and, frankly, didn't carry his weight. There followed one trip which I cannot erase from memory.

It was a four-man trip with two guns, "Moose" and I and two others. I had been with Moose before. He was a big, good-natured lad with large brown eyes—hence the name "Moose." With me, he had a tendency to do whatever I suggested. At this location there was no dugout, just a funkhole where two might crawl in for shelter. There was a good dugout ten minutes' walk away. To get some rest, we agreed that two could take the day shift and two the night shift, alternately, three days apiece. Moose and I took the night shift the first three days.

One excellent gun emplacement was beside a curving railway embankment. Behind the pit was a heavy shelter of logs and stones. We kept up a regular nightly strafe. As usual, we had orders to fire so many shells every 24 hours. Although the Stokes fired only a ten-pound shell, it was designed for rapid fire. Two men working together, pulling safety pins and dropping shells down the barrel could put half a dozen shells in the air before the first one hit the ground. The enemy didn't like us and did his best to put us out of business. He sent over quite heavy shells but most exploded against the embankment. If we stepped back under the shelter, we were relatively safe.

The second gun was placed in a shallow pit 50 yards up the trench from the other one. The pit was too shallow; there was no protection. Like those before us, we placed the gun there and set it on the S.O.S. line, the enemy's front line, but never expected to fire from that position. S.O.S., by the way, was a signal. We interpreted it as "Save Our Souls." It meant that the infantry needed immediate support, usually because the enemy was attacking.

The situation worked fine for three nights. Then Moose and I took the day shift and retired at night to the good dugout. Months before, I had written home for my old telescope. By chance, I had just received it. (I still have it though it's a little the worse for wear). Moose and I had all day to study the gun positions. We seldom fired by day. We wanted to know just how effective our fire was. After some discussion, we worked out a routine. Moose would take the telescope and walk around the trenches to another observation post where a section of brick wall was still standing with a brick conveniently knocked out at the bottom. From there, he had a good view of the enemy front line. I timed him. In 12 minutes, I sent a shell over. Moose came back to report. It dropped at the front line but would be more effective if it was a little to the left to hit where the communication trench joins the front line. We repeated, and I wrote down our findings for future use. This was a game but it made life more interesting.

The last night of the trip was different. Moose had made a spot of tea on a charcoal brazier for supper and we were about ready to settle for the night. I was near the steps and heard the machine guns open up. I was sensitive to that. When the machine guns started like that, there was usually trouble. I ran up the steps in time to see a bright green flare in the forward area. I yelled at Moose, "S.O.S." With rifles and equipment dangling, we ran down the trench. The ten-minute walk ended in about three. Moose had longer legs and was a bit ahead.

Instead of stopping at the S.O.S. gun, Moose went right ahead and joined the other two lads. I was a little annoyed but there was no use following; I'd only be in the way. I dropped into the shallow pit of the S.O.S. gun, pulled the pins and dropped shells down the barrel as fast as I could, pausing only to traverse right and left, so all the shells wouldn't fall in the same place. Some enemy shells came so close, they took my breath away. After months of frustration, this was my big moment. Whiz bangs screamed past. I was head and shoulders above ground. Chunks of iron whizzed around; I heard them. Some fell in the pit. I heard them in spite of the general row. One shell hit the gun and bounced off. I seemed to have a charmed life. It was all over in ten minutes. The air was full of smoke and dust, but I was so intent that I continued firing until Moose came along and suggested it was time to quit.

We made a count in daylight and found we had fired almost 150 rounds from the two guns in about five minutes. Next day, we got a report of the raid. There were no casualties in our front line. Our lads had taken three prisoners and none of the rest of the raiding party got away. It had been an enemy failure. There was even a kind word for the Stokes gun support.

After five days, we were relieved at night by one of our own gun crews and went back to Lievins for five days. I went to a dressing station with sore legs from impetigo that caused deep sores, irritated by marching. The C.S.M. gave me light duty, doing guards and fatigues at headquarters.

When we returned to the line, we were on the same guns as before. The previous crew had done some work. No. 2 gun was in a better position and shells were protected from shrapnel with sandbags. Our crew dug a funk hole in the side of the trench to give us some protection. Of course, we drew some return fire. Our position being mid-way between the front line and support line trenches, we got the shorts and overs. Our two guns were fairly active both day and night.

For two consecutive nights, we "Stood to" all night because

an enemy attack was expected. Our orders were simple enough: "Fire your guns as long as you can and then don't forget you have rifles." Heroic words from a guy who wasn't sticking around to see his orders carried out!

TIME OUT IN HOSPITAL

The impetigo sores on my legs were getting worse. I got to a dressing station and received salve and bandages and had "light duty" for a time. I did odd jobs but found time to publish a newspaper, "The Stokesville Eyeopener." (Name copied from a Calgary newspaper.) It was handprinted on a large sheet of paper and pinned on the battery notice board, attracting a lot of attention from both officers and men, for in it I put all the jokes I had heard about individuals in the battery. At least there was something to laugh about. But when it reached the fourth edition, some of the lads had added crude jokes of their own for which I got blamed. The Stokesville Eyeopener folded up!

After Lens, the battery went out for a rest that lasted into March. My legs got worse before the battery went back in the line, so I missed that trip. My legs were painful from marching and other activities and I was really ill. I went to a dressing station for help but the medical officer packed me into an ambulance to a field hospital at Fresnicourt, several miles back. I was there for over two weeks, on pills, sulphur ointment and bandages. The food, a diet I suppose, was ample but like hospitals everywhere, was nothing to write home about.

When I finally returned to the battery in the middle of April, they were out for a rest. Then it was back to the line.

As the front line trenches, ours and his, were still far apart, we remained in the front line by day. At night, we went to a forward position about 600 yards so our guns could reach the Hun front line. One night, we went to this forward and fired, in all, 30 rounds. The Huns seemed to have the same idea, for from somewhere he replied with trench mortars. Like us, his fire was spread all over the landscape and I couldn't see that anyone was doing more than making a noise. We were firing at where the Huns were supposed to be, using the North Star as a guide for direction. It was not always so. We usually tried to get off registering shots in daylight and used the information for night firing.

The Huns continued intermittently to strafe our front line with 4.1's. We had to spend some time in our funk hole, an open shelter with a strip of iron and a layer of sandbags on top. In the afternoon we made a trip to the forward area to insert detonators in the ammunition for night firing. Another trip around midnight was made to fire some 40 rounds from our forward gun.

When we were relieved and sent back to headquarters, I was again sent to Carency to help with the rations. Following the mules over Vimy means a long walk. The road from Carency means a trip over the Lens-Arras road and then up and over the Ridge on a winding road ending with a trip in the dark on the Merricourt road. After the first trip, I managed to borrow a bicycle. That worked okay, but it was so slow returning in the dark that I might as well have walked. I guess I was one of the few who went over Vimy Ridge on a bicycle.

Late in April, I was again on a sacrifice gun with two others. The gun was placed in a shell hole well out in front of the front line. Not very exciting. We slipped out in the dark of the early morn, carrying the gun and shells and had to stay there until it was dark enough at night to leave. Practically, we couldn't move and had to sit all day. We were not to fire unless attacked and couldn't stand up or we would be knocked down. To have a smoke, we had to lie in the bottom of the hole to avoid detection by the enemy.

Early in May, I was on another gun in an old emplacement. There was a fair but small dugout but it had been raining and the roof leaked! The Huns were firing over some Fish-tails, a small trench mortar, all shrapnel, not too serious. We were closer to his front line in this position.

We fired mostly at night. The afternoons were spent in the dugout entrance because it was too wet below. The Huns banged away at us with 4.1's. Iron was flying all around. I guess we are on one of his targets. We were warned to expect an enemy gas attack that didn't come off. Our lads put over a big "projector" attack at night. I don't suppose the Huns liked it but they made no reply. After that, we got heavy rains and both sides were pretty quiet.

May 6, 1917

Tonight, I am sent to the 11th Canadian Light Trench Mortar Battery. It marks a new epoch in my military "career." I am to take part in a special platoon stunt and don't know how long it will last.

On May 8, we were relieved at 2:00 a.m. by the Argyle and Sutherland Highlanders, straight from Egypt. We moved out to Villers Chatel by lorry for a ten-day rest. It turned into a longer rest than expected. We were marched with our Apple-carts to Dieval and billeted in a barn—with straw!

FLYING CORPS APPLICATION

Early in May, the sergeant who handled Captain Black's correspondence brought me a form to fill in, an application for commission in the Flying Corps. I filled it in, giving age, fitness, education and length of service. I heard nothing more for quite a while.

We did a few trips in the line in May. For two of these, I was with the guns but it proved to be a quiet front. Then I got a surprise. The captain told me he had recommended me to the 87th Battalion for a commission. He intimated that I might expect to go before the brigadier before long.

On May 30, I was sent to an interview with the colonel of the 87th Battalion at Valhoun. I had quite forgotten that I still belonged to the 87th and was merely on loan to the 11th Light Trench Mortar Battery. The interview was brief. The colonel asked a few questions and signed my application. I rode six kilometers on a borrowed bike to have that done. Captain Black's letter to the colonel was left open and I had permission to copy it. This is it:

> C.S.766   30/5/18
>
> 30-377   O.C. 87th Batt.   Ref. T 3191
>
> 842176 – Pte. Willans, L.

During the 12 months that the marginally noted O.O. has been on the strength of this unit, he has performed all his duties in an exemplary manner and his conduct has left nothing to be desired.

The only reason he has not received promotion has been because of there being so many good men senior to him on the roster. I should feel justified in recommending him for a commission in the Flying Corps.

(sgd.)   A.Black, Capt.,

Cmmdg.

11th Can. L.T.M.Battery

It was so seldom that one got a kind word in the army that I valued this letter, at the time, more than the questionable prospect of the Flying Corps.

For most of June, we had been in the line. Nothing more seemed to happen about the Flying Corps. I almost forgot about the whole matter. We were now on the Arras front. I had three trips with the guns, but the front was a quiet one with the enemy far away, out of range for the most part.

In the middle of June, I received an order to visit a nearby town to come before the brigadier. I hitch hiked and found the place and reported at his office. This was Brigade Major Odlum. He was living on a French estate. The sergeant at the office directed me to a summerhouse.

The brigadier, an older man, was of course, a big shot to me. He asked the usual questions. Finally, we had quite a conversation. It ended with him signing a recommendation that I be considered for a commission in the Flying Corps. He sorted out my papers and promised that he would forward them to the Flying Corps Command.

SPANISH FLU

We came out of the line at the end of June. On July 1, I became deathly ill. I lay on some straw in a French barn, unable to move for two days. I had plenty of company. There were a dozen of us lying side by side. A doctor came around daily, taking pulse and temperature and giving each man a couple of pills—aspirin, I supposed, the only pills the army had for what ails you. The illness was called "Spanish Flu." We had heard of the large number of deaths in Britain from this flu. Our boys were very ill for a few days but I didn't hear of any deaths.

A friend, who was too tough to get the flu, certainly looked after me. Each meal time, he took both mess tins and got them filled, one for "poor Len." Of course, I couldn't stand the smell of food so he got double rations. I wasn't too sick to be amused. The third day, I had some tea. The next day, I was hungry!

After the first week of July, the long rest was over. We cleaned our guns, ready for something. Then we moved by rail to dugouts east of Arras. It seemed unnaturally quiet. Only our guns were busy.

A week later, it was the Ballieul Front. Three of us were on gun in reserve position in an old cement gun-pit. We were not allowed to fire although our field guns were busy night and day. The Huns opened up with a little hate once in a while: whiz-bangs, 4.1's and big overhead bursts.

We were getting used to the daily strafes. The three of us crouched in the little pill-box behind the gun and waited until it was over. But one day, the Huns broke the rules. They hit our pill-box with something that knocked us silly. At night, next time away from the line, I went with the ration party to meet the mule train coming in. Just as we got the mules unloaded, the Huns landed about fifteen 6.9's around the dump. There was nowhere to hide; we just stayed there and took it. I was glad to get back with a whole skin.

FLYING CORPS INTERVIEW

Late in July, we went back in the line for about two weeks. I did one trip with the guns. On the 24th, I had orders to go to Aubigny for an interview with a Flying Corps officer. I hitchhiked and found the place. Around 20 others were there for the same purpose. Interviews went on all afternoon. Finally, my turn came. This English officer seemed more interested in whether or not the applicant was what he considered a "gentleman." But his methods were peculiar.

This chap was particularly nasty. He accused me of a number of things. I was silent until he asked a direct question and then answered in the negative. He accused me of questioning the previous applicants of their interview. I denied this truthfully. Then he said, "You must have heard all the talk that is going on out there?" "Certainly, sir, but I was not impressed by that talk." He then asked about my education. I replied truthfully but volunteered nothing. Had I told him I had left school at 11 years of age, I should have been sunk.

"Are you familiar with geometry?" "Yes, sir, but sketchy." "What is an isosceles triangle?" "A triangle with three equal sides." "And what else?" I was stuck. He added, "And three equal angles." "That, sir, is the logical corollary to my reply." I felt superior to this fellow in spite of his gold braid.

Then he switched. "Do you know the Morse Code?" "Yes, sir." I didn't tell him that I knew the Morse Code was then used in flying and that I had spent hours in trench and dugout, learning it backwards and forwards. This, apparently, was his clincher. He didn't know the little diary, my source of the code, was still in my tunic pocket. He shot at me in rapid succession:

"What is T?" "Umpty."

"H?' "Iddy, iddy iddy iddy."

"B?" "Umpty, iddy iddy."

"What is the figure 3?" "Iddy, iddy, iddy, umpty, umpty."

He quit that, probably thinking I knew the Morse Code better than he did.

His next question could have been dangerous to me. He asked, "Did you attend Grammar School?" Without hesitation, I replied, "We don't call them Grammar Schools in Canada. I did attend a continuation class after passing Public School." I was well aware that "Public School" meant something different in England—the school of the elite. And I failed to tell him that I lasted only six months in the continuation class because of pneumonia and only retained a knowledge of typing and a little Pitman shorthand. I think the interrogator was out of his depth. In a slightly more reasonable manner, he said, "Well, we'll give you a chance." "Thank you, sir!" I left without knowing whether I was a success or a failure. Nor did I care much. If I were to associate with blokes like him, I would rather stay with the battery.

Immediately after I returned to the battery, we were pulled out of the line in a hurry. We went several miles south by train and then marched from one little town to another. On the way, we passed a camp of Yanks who were now on the line. That would be the Chateau-Thierry front. We marched with guns in carts, wearing greatcoats in rain and shine from 10:00 p.m. until noon on August 6. Fourteen hours on a march said to be between 30 and 40 kilometers. I only know it was a darn long march.

The battle for Amiens, which commenced August 8, 1918, was the beginning of the last Hundred Days for World War 1. August 8 was described in history books as Germany's Black Day. It was the beginning of the end. I knew nothing of these fancy designations at that time. I knew only that August 8 was the longest day of my life, mindful of the time when the sun stood still for Joshua way back in Genesis days. For me, it was two 24-hour days rolled into one. For a long time after, it was a bad dream and made me wonder why I was still alive.

Back around the first of July 1918, we heard rumours that we were moving south to the Arras front. Arras, we remembered, was the southern edge of the Vimy Ridge affair. But no rumour ever suggested what we were going to do next. On July 11, we went into the line east of Arras, were out a few days and then back on the same front. We came out of the line the night of July 31. August 3, we commenced a journey that led us to Ameins. We travelled around 100 kilometers by truck to Cannesseres, said to be 42 kilometers S.W. of Ameins. Later, we left all surplus kits, including greatcoats, in a barn in a village called Berneville. I guess mine is still there. I never saw it again.

We left Berneville on the afternoon of August 6 and spent the night in a wood amid a jumble of guns and tanks. A lot of machinery was being organized for the fray. On the night of August 7, we were again on the move. We marched through a part of Ameins, through a wrecked city and sat in trenches awaiting the dawn and the attack.

We found that one Stokes gun with 12 shells and a crew of seven was attached to each infantry platoon. We were to support in case of counter-attack. This was our first experience with open warfare. It had been a year of trenches. This was a big change. We had no definite instructions, just go ahead and do what was necessary but save the shells for counter-attack.

We huddled together for warmth. It was damp and cold toward dawn and we were lightly clad. A damp rubber sheet is not a warm garment. At dawn, the guns opened up and we started to march. Tanks roared past us as the barrage opened up. Rumour said there were 500 tanks in this action. The thunder of the opening barrage and the roar of machinery made too much noise for us to hear the spoken word.

We went down a hill and crossed a fast-flowing river, perhaps the headwaters of the Somme, on a pontoon bridge of beer barrels and planks. Some of the barrels were holed by shrapnel and had become sinkers instead of buoys. A dead mule lay on one corner and we hopped along trying to keep our feet dry as the bridge gave under our increased weight. Some dead troops lay on the near side. Some enemy shells were landing on both sides of us and the acrid stink of high explosive was heavy in the air. We ascended a rise to miles of level country.

Our party had seven men. One, a corporal, was an old friend of mine. We were to go along with an infantry platoon, of what battalion I never knew. It didn't seem to matter. We had a Stokes Gun and 12 shells. We would be no use in the advance but were there to use our gun in event of a counter-attack.

We were heavily loaded. The gun barrel weighed 60 pounds, the legs 35 and the base-plate about 40. Twelve ten-pound shells added another 120 pounds. The Stokes' shells were the awkward load. Two sand-bags tied together, each containing three shells, made it possible for a man to carry the extra 60 pounds. And of course, we had our rifles and ammunition. Each man carried a load and those without specific loads carried the extra rifles. We continually switched loads. Sometimes I had the 60-pound barrel or base plate or legs or three rifles. The load became a killer for we had to keep up with the lighter clad infantry.

As we eased our loads into that reserve trench, we realized that we were back in the infantry with a vengeance, with preposterous things to carry and perhaps no opportunity to use all this heavy hardware.

Still in single file, we went through trenches and around shell holes. But the real war was still far to the front of us. The advance at this time was going on about as fast as we were moving. We passed some of our artillery with all guns firing. The enemy was hitting back and several heavy shells came that way. As we were passing one battery, some big ones came over. They were close and we instinctively hit the dirt. Out of the smoke we hurried on. All were anxious to get away from that area. A few minutes later and a couple of hundred yards farther, we counted heads. One was missing. We had last seen him just before those last shells arrived. But this was a job where there was no turning back. The army adage, "Look out for number one," became a grim reality. With him gone, six of our Stoke's shells had gone. (We heard later that he was in a field hospital, seriously wounded.)

Our long day had only just begun. The sun was high and our loads were getting heavier but the front line was still well in front. We had started at dawn and plodded slowly, interrupted by occasional shellfire. I glanced at my watch. It was exactly 11:00 A.M. when our lot became the front line.

A line of infantry, facing distant machine gun fire, was digging in. We dropped into the shallow trenches and lay a few minutes while signals were exchanged up and down the line. Then our young officer gave a wave of his arm and we were on our way. We were the front line. Right and left, as far as we could see, we were part of a ragged line, each man two or three yards from his fellow, all with rifles and bayonets at the "high port."

It was like taking part in a play. I think I said to myself, "Am I really here?"

Scared? Actually, no. There was victory in the air. The enemy was on the run. He was fighting a rear-guard action. It was like a giant movie on an endless screen. We were hungry, thirsty, sore with our loads, but young and strong. There was no time to think. We were on our way. The enemy had been forced out of his trenches. We had passed some captured enemy guns, deserted alongside piles of ammunition. We had passed prisoners on their way to the cages. You absorbed these details as you passed. It all had its effect.

We were spread out in a long line over open land like bald prairie. We faced a mile or so of open field. The ground was hard and dry. The sun was now overhead and hot. The grass was only a couple of inches high. There was no natural cover in our part of the line. There was distant machine gun fire. A young officer was leading us with hand signals, "up" and "down." We would advance a little, then down-up-down.

Most that came our way were ricochets, hitting the ground and bouncing. When a burst of fire came your way, they buzzed like a swarm of bees. We would advance about 30 yards. The signal would be "down." We flopped. Then up and a few yards more. Other groups were doing the same all along the line. We crossed a shallow trench hastily dug by the enemy and then abandoned.

Now we came under heavy direct machine gun fire. It was tragic. I saw men who failed to get up on the signal. I saw others fall. I was separated from our crew, lost all sight of signals and just did what the rest did. As I scrambled to my feet on one occasion, I noticed an infantryman next to me. I was carrying three rifles at the time and had trouble getting to my feet. This chap got up as I did—he was six feet away. I glanced back and saw him stumble, then roll over, dead! (It was a standing order not to stop for wounded. There were stretcher bearers following us.)

We were advancing too fast. The fire was coming from a village on a hill to our left. The line in front of the village had slowed up. We got the signal to retire. We scrambled back to the bit of trench and crowded into it. Earlier, we had passed some captured Hun howitzers with our lads getting ready to use them. They had turned them around and were preparing the ammunition. Otherwise, we had no visible artillery support. There were no tanks left in our part of the line.

An enemy gun from somewhere got our range and sent over three or four shells uncomfortably close. As the smoke rose, we got the signal to advance. We hurried on about 50 yards or so and down again. The machine gun fire was wicked. When a machine gun bullet hit the sod a yard or so in front of your face and bounced over your head, it tore a "piece of pie" the size of your hand out of the sod. Once in a while, this piece of sod hit you in the face. Then you began hiding behind your tin hat with your nose in the grass roots. Even if the piece of pie missed, you got some of it. You were breathing through your mouth and got a mouthful of sand and gravel. You were panting from heat and exhaustion and the result was unpleasant. Apart from the possibility of sudden death, we suffered from thirst. Under the excitement (not the least of which was the thrilling evidence that the enemy was on the run) and the hot August sun, water bottles were soon empty.

We were up again and down again. We had a bad hour. Every time we moved, it seemed someone failed to get up. In one of these rushes, the man second on my right failed to get up. He had rolled over, face up. I was still alive and moving. I hadn't time to think of him again.

A Hun gun got our range and sent some shells too close for comfort. We got the order to advance. We hurried forward a few yards. Down! Up! Ahead and down again. Without looking back, you knew we had left several behind.

Just when life had become most grim, a miracle happened. Cavalry! I didn't know we had such things. During the long trench warfare, I failed to realize that there was cavalry in training. These were Canadians, about 20. Some carried lances with pennants (for signaling); all had machine guns and bags of bombs and extra horses. They slowed up to go through our line and then were off at a lope along a little valley in front of us. It was only a matter of minutes, and the machine gun fire from the village on our left ceased. God bless those boys with the horses!

In less than ten minutes, we were on our way. No machine gun fire! It was like magic. I had to reassess my opinion of trained horses and men. The cavalry had obviously encircled the village on our left and settled accounts with the machine gunners. We passed one dead horse. I knew the rider would not leave a wounded horse. He had to shoot it.

We followed down the valley. The village on our left was

silent.

We plodded on for about half an hour unopposed. Then an enemy anti-tank gun went into action. We seemed to be moving directly toward this gun which kept up a fairly steady stream of these wicked little shells in front of our line, trying to slow our advance. The armored nose-caps, which made a shallow hole in the dry sod, screamed over followed by a shower of gravel and stones. It was nasty but apparently not effective. The line moved on whether we liked it or not. Ahead of us was the chalk cliff of a road cutting. As we got close to it, the shellfire ceased. The gun no longer could reach us. By the time we reached the road, some ambulances and lighter vehicles were pulling up in the shelter of the cliff. The line on our right had moved faster than us. On our right, a bit over half a mile away, was an open road leading back towards Amiens, unobstructed, except for enemy fire

The road led to a plateau behind the little village. On our right front was a large town, a mile or so away. We could see some of our transport moving toward the town. We kept plodding along toward the crossroad, but an enemy anti-tank gun fired some wicked little shells, always in front of us, a delaying action. The shells tore small, small holes sprinkling us with dirt. Up, down and ahead was the road. The gun suddenly quit, probably attacked from the rear.

We reached the crossroad where our lot turned left behind the little village and spread out on the open ground. From our position, we could watch the infantry digging in. We saw a figure walking in front of the line. A distant machine gun was sweeping the area. We were getting our share of it but were sheltered by our gun pit. "Who is that so-and-so?" someone muttered. He was identified to us as the "The Major." He wore a kilt and carried a cane and walked up and down on a 300-yard front as the men were digging in. We watched him for some time, swinging his cane as if on a parade ground. He continued until the light failed. Even under our circumstances, we could not but applaud such cool courage

An enemy battery was shelling the village behind us. (We were now in front of the village the cavalry had earlier taken.) The sun was low and everything that moved was silhouetted against that ball of fire. The infantry were digging in for the night. We chose a vacant gun pit about 100 yards behind them and set up our gun. We counted heads. All had arrived and with a complete gun and six shells. We still didn't know about the seventh missing man.

At dark, Moose made a trip down to the infantry and reported they were staying for the night and would let us know when to join them. We had some stale sandwiches we'd brought with us. We were more tired than hungry but we had no water. Each one was the same. During the heat of the day, all had taken the occasional nip and all bottles were empty. This was serious; mention water and all were thirsty.

When it was about dark, two of us went in search of water. We crossed the road into the town behind us. Occasional enemy shells were falling in and around the town. We found one well with a pump and a long line waiting to use it. We joined the line but as we grew accustomed to the darkness, we decided that at the rate the line was moving, it would take most of the night to get water. We decided to go back and think of something better. Before we got far, a salvo of three shells fell on the road ahead. We hurried to pass the spot before the gunners tried again. The shells had got a party on the road. We paused. Men and mules were piled in a heap. None were alive. The road wasn't a healthy place to hang around.

But the road was wet. It had been a water party. There were cans of water. Most had leaked out but we got what we could carry—each got two two-gallon cans. It was flavoured with mud and gasoline but it was gorgeous!

At the gun, the boys were considering a search party, thinking we might have been caught by those shells. We arranged for one man to stay on guard, ate our stale sandwiches, and filled up on cold water. We were too tired to be alive.

Later, Moose and one of the boys went forward to visit the infantry and find out what we were expected to do. He came back with the story that we had not taken our objective and that the advance would continue in the morning. No time was set. We would be notified. This news ended the first day.

The events of the previous day prevented much sleep. We slept a bit in turn but were ready to move when the word was given. We waited for the signal which did not come. Just before dawn, Moose crept forward to see what was happening. He came back worried. "The boys have gone." There was only one thing to do—follow them.

Shouldering our loads, we commenced a six-man advance into the unknown. As it became light, we saw a town a couple of miles away on our right front. Some shells were falling there, but we couldn't know whose shells. We saw some movement on the Amiens road toward the town. Away to the right on some higher ground, we could see French troops advancing in line. Their blue uniforms and long frog-sticking bayonets glistened in the morning sun. Another surprise! We were now on rising ground and could see no sign of our troops. We decided that they had swung to the right attacking the town which was now clearly visible. We edged in that direction.

As we went on, there was some scattered machine gun fire. Then the fire came too close for comfort. It appeared we were the target. We scrambled into a piece of trench. It proved to be a network of trenches which didn't seem to lead anywhere. One arm led toward the town on our left. We followed it for a bit. But this also proved unhealthy. The stream of bullets infiltrated the trench. We went forward on hands and knees. We wondered if we should set up our gun and walk back but decided against it. We had no idea whether the enemy gun was 500 or 1000 or 2000 yards away.

Since we had started our six-man advance, we had changed direction quite a lot and were confused. We really did not know who was holding the town. From the sound of firing, we judged that it was still disputed territory. Also, our own troops might be in that direction. We came to the end of the trench and saw some trees on the edge of the town only 50 yards away and decided to make a run for it, one at a time. Moose went first. When I saw him disappear among the trees, I went. I tried to ignore the screaming bullets, but with our loads, it was not a run but a walk. I threw myself flat under the trees. It proved to be an orchard of small trees leafed almost to the ground. The machine gun bullets crashed through the trees like hail on a tin roof. I had no pride. I crawled.

We seemed to be in a cul-de-sac with no way out. A high brick wall was on our left, buildings in front and another wall further right. We found a back door to the house in front. We entered, rifles at the ready, for we still didn't know whether this was enemy territory or ours. The door led to a basement room which it was empty, a Hun canteen. In the dim light, we saw nothing but tobacco and cigarettes, nothing to eat.

I grabbed a large paper carton of cigarettes and shoved it under a shoulder strap. In the dim light, we found a stairway leading up. In an open door to the street lay a Hun officer past caring. I unhooked his water bottle and snapped it on my belt. (I still have it!) The fool things you will do when your mind's in a whirl! We still didn't know where we were.

We went through a house and came out on a street. Machine gun fire was coming down the street with bullets bouncing from the walls. We saw a sign, "Battn. H.Q." on the farther side of the street. We crossed. The sign was over a cellar entrance. Moose and I went inside; the rest waited. An officer was sitting at a table under an electric light. We saluted. Moose was winded or tongue-tied. As usual, I was spokesman and said, "Sir, we are trench mortar men reporting." I was about to explain how we had been left behind but didn't get a chance. The officer said, "Fine. Just what we are looking for." Glancing at his map, he said, "Go up this street, the one leading east. There is a machine gun giving us a bit of trouble. See if you can silence it." This was a quick turn of events. But an order was an order. We still had a gun and six shells. We went out and told the others.

I don't know how the others felt, but I know I thought we should be doing something to justify our existence. We had lugged that gun and our half dozen shells for a day and a half and here was our chance to strike a blow. Nothing heroic about this. Just fed up with carrying these loads.

We tried. But these little French towns, like Topsy, "just growed." The buildings were evidently built before there were roads; streets were then put in to accommodate the buildings. A jog or two in the main street was not unusual. This was no exception. We proceeded as told, hugging the south side of the street because machine gun bullets in little bursts of fire were bouncing off the buildings and road on the opposite side. When we reached the "jog" where the street took a one-eighth turn to the south, we were right in the path of that distant machine gun. We tried to get around the corner one at a time, but there was no cover in sight. The chance of staying alive for even 50 yards seemed remote and apparently there were 500 yards to go. We stayed a short time but the situation didn't alter.

Moose and I talked it over and decided to try some other way. There must be another street on the other side of these houses. We poked along behind some buildings, a courtyard, and an alley and came out on another street. It was quiet there and in a few minutes, we had reached the last of the buildings on the edge of the town. While looking for a place to set up our gun, we came across one of our own trench mortar crews with one of our own officers in charge. We explained the orders we had received. Our officer said, "We have tried, but the machine gun is way out of range. Dig a gun-pit and put your gun in S.O.S. position." The Army thinks of everything. Somewhere in the book it says, "Obey the last order first." In the Army, you learn to do as you are told.

What made things more attractive was that the boys had a fire started and were making tea. They shared rations with us and we began to live again. After eating, I sampled the Hun officer's bottle. It contained some sort of peach brandy, not my cup of tea, so I passed it around and got it back empty. The carton of cigarettes, still wedged under my shoulder strap, I sampled and threw away—cabbage leaves!

The machine gun fire had slowed up; our infantry was dug in on the edge of the town. I have a memo that says the name of the town is Quesnel, which was said to be our objective. It was also said that the two-day advance had been ten miles. Before dark, we were relieved and moved back several kilometers to what had been the enemy horse lines and camped there in the open. That was the evening of August 9. The long day was over.

There was but little rest. There was some enemy long-range shellfire and a flurry of night bombing. We had to dig in for shelter. One stray shell landed behind our camp and killed a horse.

It was there that we were introduced to one of the ghastly things about war. It is one of those things you seldom talk about. A few hundred yards from our camp was a marquee which we had passed on the previous day. It housed an enemy hospital, and attendants had remained with their patients during the attack. The hospital was respected but our mopping-up squads removed the staff as prisoners. It was understandable. During the attack, we could not afford to leave enemy personnel behind our thinly held line. By the time we reached there, some of the wounded had died and the rest were in bad shape. Some of our lads had been carrying water to them—the only help they could give. It gives one pause. What price victory!

We remained in the same spot until the August 14—five days. It wasn't a comfortable rest period. We had left all but our fighting equipment far behind and had no greatcoats. The nights were cold after the heat of the day. Our battery was told that we were to go back in the line that night.

We were lined up for dinner on the fourth day, when Captain Black came along and handed me a large envelope. "This," he said, "Contains your documents for the Flying Corps and pass to Blighty. You will report to the town major at Ailly-sur-Somme." I was stunned for a moment. Recent events had knocked all thought of the Flying Corps out of my head.

I had been recommended for a commission in the Flying Corps months before, but as I heard no more about it, I thought it a dead issue. I gathered my wits and said, "Where is Ailly-sur-Somme?" "Follow the main road. It is about twenty miles." I ate my stew; I would need that. The cooks excelled themselves with a couple of sandwiches. The boys crowded around, patting me on the back and asking questions and wishing me the best. I didn't see Old Hitch. He was away somewhere. I wrote to him later, and continued letters through the years. I was off! I was happy to go but bitten by the idea that I was letting our side down.

I walked about three miles down the road, travelling light, my pack and greatcoat were gone. I still had my rifle; that is a personal thing you don't part with. A lorry came from behind and slowed up to let me climb behind, took me a couple of miles, and slowed up to let me off before turning onto a side road. I walked a few miles more. A lorry came behind with one driver. He invited me to sit in the spare driver's seat and got to know my history. He took me a full ten miles before I started walking again. That's the way I got to Ailly-sur-Somme, just another village on the Somme River.

This was August 14, 1918. I was due for some shocks. The first was upon arriving at Ailly-sur-Somme. I found the town major's office. Couldn't miss it—the only office on the one main street. I realized, with a jolt, I was now in the British Army! I had lost my nationality.

The chap in charge of the office was older. Regular army, I should guess, and had at last gotten a cushy job. I suppose he was a corporal. All was routine. He told me where the billet was, a barn in the near distance. He was absolutely neutral. I handed him my documents. He turned them over a couple of times and handed them back. I figured he couldn't read. He was polite but not cordial. I'd had a long day and was hungry and tired. I asked where I could get something to eat. He stared at me and said that meals would be provided. I persisted and he grudgingly admitted that there was a "Y" near the billet. As I was leaving, he said, "You will parade at eight tomorrow to leave for Boulogne." He probably regarded me privately as another of those "bloody Canadians." He was a lunk as far as I was concerned.

I found the "Y." After I had stood for a few minutes, a bored individual appeared. "No, we don't serve meals. We have cigarettes and tobacco and some tinned goods." I bought a pack of cigarettes, English poison, and some sweet biscuits. I ate the biscuits on the way to the barn.

There were around a dozen lads there, all English. I was regarded as something dropped from outer space. We finally got supper and, as I was an unknown quantity and probably hadn't been raised properly, and there was a long evening ahead, I went for a walk.

The Somme River was 100 yards across a field. I wandered over. I met a very young officer who had charge of a group of English lads and had brought them down for a swim. This officer was very pleasant. When he found that I had just come out of the Amiens Battle, he wanted to hear all about it. With it fresh in my mind, I gave a vivid account of what I knew. He was greatly interested, at once proud and horrified, and had me repeat a lot of things. He said, "I hear you had tanks?" I admitted that tanks, as we called them, had been used but that I had seen only one and that it was standing with its nose in the air when it failed to get across a trench. (Nothing to do with the tanks of later years—these were in the experimental stage.)

When the conversation lagged, I intimated that I was going to have a swim and started to undress. My officer friend expostulated, "Oh, my dear fellow, you mustn't go in without a costume!" I had made a faux pas and apologized. We were a long way from human habitation and I saw nothing wrong. The officer sent one of his boys for a "costume." It had been a long time since I was in swimming. The water was cold and deep and the current swift. I paddled around for a while, got chilled and crawled out. I had the sense to wash and wring out the costume before returning it with appreciation, expressed my "Au revoir" and hurried back to the barn, for light was failing. I made friends with some of the lads but was still regarded as a curiosity. Some were going on leave and some were there for other reasons. Not one was going to the Flying Corps.

We had breakfast at seven and parade at eight. It was the British Army all right! A severe sergeant had us fall in, in two ranks, then "Shun! - Stand at ease!" three or four times. We marched off to "Left, right, left and hip, hip, hip," for a quarter of a mile. It was like an exaggerated church parade.

I hadn't done that stuff since I left Valcartier. After all this fuss and bother, while the sergeant paced up and down to make sure none escaped, an engine came and pulled our box car to Boulogne. We crossed to Folkstone and then to Waterloo Station (London). It was evening and too late to report to the Flying Corps, so I felt on my own.

I did stop at the Waterloo information desk and inquired the address of the Flying Corps headquarters. The young lady laughed at me and said, "In Hampstead , right across Hampstead Heath. But it isn't the Flying Corps. It is now the Royal Air Force." I explained that I had just come from France where we hadn't heard of the change. I knew my way around this part of London and got a bed at the Maple Leaf Club and more important, a good supper. Somewhere en route, I have forgotten where, I ran into a paymaster and received two pounds; otherwise, I would have been broke.

I wrote a note to Arthur to let him know where I was. Away back, while I was in the mule lines at Carency, Art, who was stationed at Cambain l'Abbe, about three miles away, visited me. One Sunday, on a borrowed bike, I called on him and had tea. He took me back, with the bike, in a side-car. Later, he wrote that he had been wounded in the left hand. Some machine gun had shattered the bones and he was months in The Prince of Wales Hospital, London, while they tried to make his hand usable. He flew again later in England but had a crash resulting in a broken nose and other injuries.

Next day, I took a tube to Hampstead and reported to the Royal Air Force. I produced my documents but nobody was interested. The papers which had caused me so much grief were a dead issue. The Canadian authorities had made all transferees to the Air Force acting sergeants with pay. The sergeant's pay was good news. I was not told to put up stripes so remained a private for all practical purposes. I was told that I was entitled to 14 days' leave and where did I want to go? I promptly said, "Ireland." I had a cousin, Willie Willans, whom I had never met. I gave his address, Bawnboy, in County Cavan. My mother was born in County Meath, not so far from there. Willie was an Anglican curate in Catholic Ireland. I was told to come back later for my travel warrant.

I wandered around all day, got something to eat at a Salvation Army and arranged for a bed. I even walked across a part of Hampstead Heath, a large, open area with small lakes and streams. But that got tiresome. It was evening when I got my warrant and night before I was out of the "red tape."

My leave started on the morrow. I got on a tube train and in ten minutes was at Lewisham, a suburb of sprawling London, where Winnie Harris and her parents lived. I had been there once before while on leave the previous December. They were excited to have me—right out of the battle they had been reading about in the papers. We talked of nothing else but my experiences; my audience was deeply interested. I left at 11:30 pm to catch the last train to London and found the Salvation Army hostel locked up. I got into a converted hotel used to house stray soldiers and slept on a wide stone window ledge since the floor was crowded. Next day, I had to wait until late afternoon for a train to Holyhead in Wales to get a late night ferry to Dublin.

LEAVE TO IRELAND

After a rough crossing of an arm of the Irish Sea, I arrived in Dublin in the early morning. Before I was allowed on the ferry, I got another shock. My rifle was taken away! We had heard of the Irish rebellion in 1916 but supposed it was over and done with. No, Dublin and the Irish were bitter. I got a receipt for the rifle and picked it up upon my return.

It was the middle of the morning before we docked. There was a shabby eating house nearby. I entered and asked for a cup of tea. A slatternly waitress appeared and looked at me as if I were something the cat dragged in, saying, "Y' cawn't have dinner till dinner time." I left, musing upon Kipling's, "Oh its Tommy this and Tommy that, and chuck him out, the brute. But it's Tommy to the rescue when the guns begin to shoot"! It was only by virtue of the British that Ireland did not become a Hun province.

I walked through what appeared to be Dublin's business section. Most public buildings were in ruins, the result of British Naval shells which settled the rebellion. I didn't meet anyone, but then I saw only a very small part of the city. I saw a sign, "Forces Welcome" and climbed some stairs to an upper room. Nothing to eat there. It was a reading and writing room. I chewed the rag with the elderly custodian until about noon. I asked where I could get dinner. He hesitated, then said, "There's a restaurant near the docks." I thanked him and left.

In the restaurant, the same frowsy abigail appeared. I thought I should assert myself. Any good opinion of the Irish had gone down the drain. I said, "Dinner, please," and chose a center table. The reply, "Tant ready" and she left. I sat it out, perhaps 20 minutes. I was the only customer. The girl came back and slapped down a plate with three large potatoes and three rashers of bacon. She returned with a couple of stale looking buns—scones, I suppose—and a mug of something black which might have been tea. I thought I had won the first round. I applied a knife to one of the spuds but it wouldn't go through because the center was not cooked. I took the hides off and used the outer portion. The bacon, however, was good. No bacon in England due to rationing but Ireland was not rationed. I bit into one of the buns and decided they were for the birds. I left without leaving a tip, a practice unheard of in England. I paid the bill, which was surprisingly small.

In the afternoon, a brief train journey to Dundalk, a junction. On the train, it was different. People talked to you, unheard of on an English train where you didn't speak to anyone unless properly introduced. At the junction, I changed to another train, one without a schedule. It was composed of two old street cars and a baggage van on a light railway, travelling at ten miles per hour. Here I met the Irish at their best. You sat opposite each other on lone seats and everybody talked. They wanted to know all my business, where I was going, where I had been and who I was visiting. It was endless but all were trying to be helpful. One man pointed to the rectory as I was getting off the train. It was visible about a mile across some fields.

There was a dirt road but it went in the wrong direction, so I started in a straight line for the rectory. After a few hundred yards across a field, I came to a wide ditch full of water. I retraced my steps. I should have known better in this land of contradiction. I followed the road which kept getting farther from my goal, but finally got to a cross road and the rectory.

When I told them who I was, I got a royal welcome from

Willie Willans and his wife, Sybil. I stayed with them most of my leave, on four meals a day, English style. For a couple of days, I cut oats with a sickle. Willie kept a horse for Sundays and grew a couple of acres of oats for the horse. He had an old hired fellow named Pat. (This world was full of Pats!) The old boy was rheumatic and couldn't cut oats but was handy at braiding straws to tie up bundles. My introduction to farming!

Willie took me to visit some of his flock. The first was an old fellow, living in one room. He had but one chair. We sat on a cot. He seemed honored by our visit. Obviously, he did all his cooking in an iron pot over a peat fire—bacon and spuds. We talk now of poverty without really knowing the meaning of the word. Another visit was to a two-room stone cottage. The housewife was delighted to have us. She immediately chased her flock of chickens out of her kitchen and dusted off two chairs for our use. I even went to church on Sunday (horse and buggy). Willie preached a good sermon to about ten people.

I saved the last two days of my leave for a trip to Portaferry to visit Mary, a correspondent I had never met. It was a longer trip than I expected. Portaferry was a little village on a lough (sea inlet), eighteen miles from Belfast in northern Ireland. At Belfast station, there was a lunch counter for troops. I accepted a cup of tea and a sandwich. I dug out some money but the volunteer waitress refused it. I insisted, but she said, "No, we don't charge anything to the boys in uniform." This was a change of atmosphere. I asked how I could get to Portaferry. "The bus leaves in the morning at eight." "Where to spend the night?" She suggested, "Temperance Hotel. The bus leaves from there." I thanked her and with further directions, found the hotel and arranged for bed and breakfast at a very reasonable sum.

I wondered how I would find Mary at Portaferry. I needn't
have worried. The bus arrival was the one event of the day
and almost the whole population of the little village was
on hand. I had dinner with Mary and her parents. In the
afternoon, Mary and I went on a little ferry to a village across
the lough where a Red Cross fete was being held. My money
had about run out, but I bought Mary a little bluebird pin as
a memento. I stayed overnight at Mary's and left for Belfast,
Dublin and London. Mary insisted that I take a lunch with
me. I was glad for that. Mary had lost a brother at the front.
He had enlisted in Canada and I visited his grave while I was
in the mule lines at Carency. Her parents, of course, had to
know all about it. We talked war half the night. I was back at
Hampstead the night my leave expired.

ROYAL AIR FORCE TRAINING

I was kept at Hampstead for a few days, billeted in one of the old houses that the Air Force had appropriated. We had a daily parade for roll call and little else. I spent my time walking about London. I even visited the London Museum but most things of interest were sandbagged in preparation for the invasion which never came. I also went to the London Zoo, of great reputation, but there was too much walking. I didn't get much beyond the monkey cage, which was really something.

The war was over for me, but I had no such idea at that time. I went into intensive training with the Royal Air Force. Mathematics, map-reading, wireless telegraphy, sending and receiving were the main subjects, with exams every second week. Stricter, sharper discipline that I had known before was the rule.

I had a physical examination and, I suppose, a mental one, too. By the merest chance, I was passed as a pilot. That was what I wanted. I was ambitious to fly a fighter plane. Such is ambition at 21! Then we were sent to St Leonard's on Sea for a disciplinary course. It was laid on thick. Polish the backs of buttons and belt buckles; pipe-clay your belt. It was all spit and polish. We were billeted in a three-story hotel on the coast. We lived about 12 in a room, on cots—temporary gentlemen. I had the indignity of being brought up on the mat for having a dirty room. I protested that, even if I was senior in service to the rest, I had no authority to make the others do up their beds properly. I won. The court, such as it was, acknowledged that I was right and promoted me to be some sort of supervisory cadet. My lads cooperated and we had no further criticism.

After two weeks at St Leonard's, we moved to Dibgate, closer to London where we got to work. We had mathematics, map reading, telegraphy and lectures on everything from deportment to geography to geology. Telegraphy was not as simple as it sounds. It meant listening day by day, to an instructor who started tapping Morse on a telegraph key, one word at a time, until we could accurately transcribe 20 words a minute. Map reading meant memorizing signs and directions on a military map and then drawing the map from memory. All depended upon paying strict attention. I suppose I got an education of a sort.

It was there I met Fatty and Culley. I was merely Len. We had to study every night so we rented a room outside of camp and spent our evening there. On Sunday, the lady made supper for us. On a sergeant's pay, I now had a little money. Fatty, the name he went by, was short and stout and a great guy with the girls. Culley was more English than Canadian. We were staunch friends and helped each other—the "three musketeers."

ARMISTICE

We had been two months at Dibgate when November 11 came, bringing the news that the war was over. Of course, I was glad it was over. At the same time, I was disappointed. I had set my goal on being a pilot and never made it. Just before November 11, I was told that I was going to work on engines and then learn to fly. You can't have everything!

On November 23, I was transferred to the Canadian camp at Shorncliffe. I got a final leave to visit my English relatives. The Canadian authorities gave me a $100.00 kit allowance, which I would have received if commissioned. I visited the store in London and picked out an officer pattern tunic and cap. But the slacks were expensive so I invested in extra towels, and underwear. I bought a pair of khaki breeches in a second-hand store to complete my uniform. In the Canadian camp, I had the rank of cadet and ate in the sergeant's mess—and paid mess dues! I was sent home after Christmas with the rank of Cadet and awarded three stripes by a grateful Canadian government.

As a grand finale, Art came to say goodbye. He was leaving for Canada. We had tea together and I bid him "bon voyage." Right after that, I was told to pack up. I sailed first class on the Acquitania, then the largest boat afloat. Then, Montreal, Kingston and Ottawa. I arrived in Ottawa a day ahead of Art and was at the station to meet him. Surprise!

At Ottawa, members of the family were on hand to meet me. My name had been published on the newspaper bulletin board. I received a delightful surprise as I stepped off the Kingston train. A girl had got past the barrier, came rushing down the platform, and kissed me. I could hardly believe it was Ollie!

(I should have written: she threw her arms around me and wouldn't let go. I had been away almost three years. Ollie was close to 19 and I had just reached 22. You were that age yourself once and perhaps can understand.)

That is the end of my story but not quite the end of my military adventures. Yes, Ollie was waiting for me when I got home. She has had a career of her own, one of waiting. She waited for me during the Great War. We were married on August 31, 1921, when she was 21. She waited for me again for five and one-half years while, with my sons, Arthur and Elwood, we toured Britain, Italy, France and northern Europe in the tail of the Fifth Canadian Armored Division. But that's another story.

Leonard Willans
WW I

Not sure when this was taken—at his enlistment or, more likely, on leave sometime during the war.

Description of *Leonard William* on Enlistment.

Apparent Age......19......years......6......months.
(To be determined according to the instructions given in the Regulations for Army Medical Service.)

Distinctive marks, and marks indicating congenital peculiarities or previous disease.
(Should the Medical Officer be of opinion that the recruit has served before, he will, unless the man acknowledges to any previous service itself, a map to that effect, for the information of the Approving Officer.)

Height......5......ft......9......ins.

Girth when fully expanded......33½......ins.
Range of Expansion......3½......ins.

Complexion......*Fresh*

Eyes......*Grey*

Hair......*Dark*

Freckles on face
mole on Right arm

Religious Denomination:
Church of England......
Presbyterian......
~~Weslyan~~ *Methodist*......
Baptist or Congregationalist......
Other Protestants......
(Denomination to be stated)
Roman Catholic......
Jewish......

CERTIFICATE OF MEDICAL EXAMINATION.

I have examined the above-named Recruit and find that he does not present any of the causes of rejection specified in the Regulations for Army Medical Services.

He can see at the required distance with either eye ; his heart and lungs are healthy ; he has the free use of his joints and limbs, and he declares that he is not subject to fits of any description;

I consider him*......*fit*......for the Canadian Over-Seas Expeditionary Force.

Date......*May 22nd*......191 6

(Sgd) *G.W.R. Smith*

Place......*Montreal Canada*

Lieut. M.C.
Medical Officer.

* "Insert here "fit" or "unfit."

Note.—should the Medical Officer consider the Recruit unfit, he will fill in the foregoing Certificate only in the case of those who have been attested, and will briefly state below the cause of unfitness i.e.;

CERTIFICATE OF OFFICER COMMANDING UNIT.

......*Leonard William*......having been finally approved and inspected by me this day, and his Name, Age, Date of Attestation, and every prescribed particular having been recorded, I certify that I am satisfied with the correctness of this Attestation.

(Sgd) *a. a. Magee* (Signature of Officer.)
Lieut. or 148th Bn.

Date......*May 26th*......191 6

Just a couple of comments about the form: note the "apparent" age for the recruit. Officials must have not been too fussy about the exact date, and I know from other stories about that era that some people didn't know their exact birthdate. Also, "Weslyan" has been crossed out and replaced with "Methodist"... must be some kind of story there. Note Grandpa's height and chest measurements; he was not a big man, always more on the slight side.

Grandpa wore his Legion blazer, hat, and medals every
November 11 in the Remembrance Day ceremonies.

Leonard Willans
1915

A dapper guy! Grandpa would have been about 18 years old in this photo.

CALENDAR 1916

Blackhall & Co., Toronto

NINE DEPARTMENTS

Department A

White and Grey Cottons, Drills, Ducks, Canton Flannels, Sheetings and Pillow Cottons, Cotton and Jute Bags, Cotton Warps and Twines, Waddings, Horse Blankets and Carriage Dusters.

Department B

Apron Ginghams, Tickings, Colored Shirtings, Saxonies, Flettes and Printed Wrapperettes.

Department C

Woollens and Tailors' Trimmings.

Department D

Dress Goods, Linings, Wash Goods and Silks.

Department E

Men's Furnishings and Lumbermen's Clothing.

Department H

Laces, Embroideries, Ribbons, Dress Trimmings, Silk, Cotton, and Linen Threads, Women's Fancy Smallwear.

Department M

Women's Furnishings, Linens and Towellings.

Department S

Smallwares, Fancy Goods, Novelties, Stationery and Wool Yarns.

Department T

House Furnishings, Blankets, Carpets, Oilcloths and Linoleums.

The actual diary Grandpa had at the beginning of the war. His notes are included in the book in different font from the main account.

...you's have neither the aesthetic melancholy, which is amusing; nor the musicians which is pedantical; nor the courtiers, which is proud; nor the soldier, which is ambitious; nor the lawyer's, which is politic; nor the lady's, which is nice; nor the lover's, which is all of these; but it is a melancholy of mine own compounded of many simples, extracted from many objects, and, indeed, the sundry contemplation of my travels, which by they ruminated wraps me in a most humorous sadness. As you like it, activ

That march of yesterday was an awful strain, especially after the route march of the night before. It was fourteen long miles with full pack. The 107th battalion was with us and they were dropping off like flies. There are a whole bunch of them on the road between Witley & Mychett. No one but a strong healthy man can stand such a walk. I only suffered from my feet; and that was because of bad boots; but I get new ones soon.

Last night the boys all got drunk — wetting the new camp. One fellow Wood — a silly kid; came around with a search-light and woke everybody up to see if they needed a shave. He stroked their chins and gave a verdict. He told me that he

CANADIAN EXPEDITIONARY FORCE
Discharge Certificate

This is to Certify that No ----842176------ (Rank)------Cadet---------------

Name (in full)----------WILLANS, Leonard -------------------- enlisted in

the---------------------148th Overseas Battalion ----------------------

CANADIAN EXPEDITIONARY FORCE at----------Montreal------ on the------22nd------

day of----MAY-----------------196.

HE served in--------Canada, England and France ----------------------

and is now discharged from the service by reason of--------DEMOBILIZATION R.O. 1343.

3DD 3- ---

THE DESCRIPTION OF THIS SOLDIER on the DATE below is as follows :—

Age --------22 yrs, 2 mths ----------   Marks or Scars ----------------------

Height-----5' 10" ------------------   ------------------------------

Complexion-----Fair-------------------   Vacc. mark left arm--------------

Eyes-----------Blue------------------   ------------------------------

Hair-----------Fair------------------   ------------------------------

L.Willans
Signature of Soldier

T.W.MacDonell
Issuing Officer

Major
Rank

Date of Discharge---February 17, 1919   O.C. Sub. Detno. #3 D.D.
Appointment

Signed at Ottawa, Ontario this 17th day of February 1919.

in Military District No--------1----------

File Reference No. 3DD 3-

N.B.—As no duplicate of this Certificate will be issued, any person finding same is requested to forward it in an unstamped envelope to the Secretary, Militia Council, Ottawa, Canada.

M P W 39a.
5000 —6-15.
H. Q. 1772-39-822.

Interesting that his height, eye colour, and hair colour have changed. The information on the form at the beginning of the war was different. I guess war changes things.

CANADIAN EXPEDITIONARY FORCE
Discharge Certificate

This is to Certify that No. ~~642170~~ (Rank) ~~Private~~

Name (in full) ~~WILLANS, Leonard~~ enlisted in

the ~~164th Overseas Battalion~~

CANADIAN EXPEDITIONARY FORCE at ~~Montreal~~ on the ~~22nd~~

day of ~~MAY~~ 1916.

HE served in ~~Canada, England and France~~

and is now discharged from the service by reason of ~~DEMOBILIZATION P.O. 1843,~~

~~SID 3.~~

THE DESCRIPTION OF THIS SOLDIER on the DATE below is as follows :—

Age ~~22 yrs, 2 mths~~	Marks or Scars
Height ~~5' 10"~~	
Complexion ~~fair~~	Vacc. mark left arm.
Eyes ~~Blue~~	
Hair ~~Fair~~	

_____
Signature of Soldier

T. W. MacDonell
Issuing Officer

Major
Rank

Date of Discharge ~~February 17, 1919~~

O.C. Sub. Depot, #3 D.D.
Appointment

Signed at ~~Ottawa, Ontario~~ this ~~17th~~ day of ~~February~~ 19 ~~19~~

in Military District No. _____

File Reference No. ~~SDD 3~~

N.B.—As no duplicate of this Certificate will be issued, any person finding same is requested to forward it in an unstamped envelope to the Secretary, Militia Council, Ottawa, Canada.

M. F. W. 33
300m.—9-18.
H.Q. 1772-30-392

14879098R00088

Printed in Great Britain
by Amazon.co.uk, Ltd.,
Marston Gate.